HOME

Chronicle of a North Country Life

H O M E

Chronicle of a North Country Life

by Beth Powning

Stewart, Tabori & Chang
New York

Originally published in 1996 by Penguin Books Canada Ltd. in Canada under the title
Seeds of Another Summer.

Library of Congress Cataloging-in-Publication Data

Powning, Beth, 1949–
    Home : chronicle of a north country life / by Beth Powning.
       p.   cm.
    ISBN 1-55670-460-7 (HC : alk. paper)
    1. Farm life--New Brunswick. 2. Country life--New Brunswick.
    3. Powning, Beth, 1949---Homes and haunts--New Brunswick.
    I. Title.
    S521.P74   1996
    818'.5403--dc20

Published in 1996 by Stewart, Tabori and Chang,
a division of U. S. Media Holdings, Inc.
575 Broadway, New York, New York 10012

Quotes from Gary Snyder (Chapters 1 and 5), *The Practice of the Wild* (San Francisco:
North Point Press, 1990).
Quote from Henry David Thoreau (Chapter 2), *Walden* (New York: Signet Classics,
1960).
Quote from Barry Lopez (Chapter 2), *Arctic Dreams* (New York: Bantam Books, 1987).
Excerpt from "From the Crest" (Chapter 3), in *Clearing*, copyright © 1974 by Wendell
Berry, reprinted by permission of Harcourt Brace & Company.
Quote from John Fowles (Chapter 4), *The Tree* (Toronto: Collins Publishers, 1979.)
Quote from Gary Snyder (Chapter 6), "Ripples on the Surface," in *No Nature* (New
York: Pantheon Books, 1992).

Printed in Singapore
10 9 8 7 6 5 4 3 2 1

To
Peter and Jacob
with love

ACKNOWLEDGMENTS

This book would not exist were it not for all the other families and their ancestors who have lived on this farm. First and foremost, I wish to acknowledge the labor and love of those who came here long before I did, and to pay my respects to the memories of this place that live on in their families.

I thank the first readers of the manuscript: Allan Cooper, Bob Osborne, Valerie Ahwee, Mary Johnson, Ruth Dorfman, Arnie and Ruth Becker, June Nelson, and especially Kathy Hooper. And I thank, in memoriam, Harry and Inez Walton, our first friends in New Brunswick; Edwin Way Teale and Nellie Teale, who inspired me as a child; and my grandparents, Roger and Helen Davis, and Sharon and Elizabeth Brown, readers and lovers of nature all.

To the organizations whose generous grants helped make this book possible, I thank you for your belief in me, and in my project: New Brunswick Department of Environment—the Environmental Trust Fund, the Fundy Model Forest Project and J. D. Irving, Ltd.

Thank you to the Department of Municipalities, Culture, and Housing; and heartfelt thanks to Charlotte Glencross. Part of this book was written at Leighton Artist Colony at The Banff Centre for the Arts. I'm grateful to all the people at the Centre who settled me into my cabin in the mountains.

Thanks to my brother, Mark Davis, who went adventuring with me in the fields of childhood; and to the poet Gary Snyder—I heard you speak of red pebbles, and it brought me home again. To Freeman Patterson: thank you for helping me come closer to the threshold. To E. L. Doctorow, who taught me that there are no rules: thank you for laying the groundwork which has supported me. And thank you, Peg Powning, my very first reader and most loyal supporter: you kept me going in dark days.

To my wonderful and most beloved parents, Wendell and Alison Davis: thank you for the inestimable gifts both of life and of a country childhood.

My deepest gratitude to my agent, Aaron Milrad: your unfailing optimism, belief in the book and tireless persistence made it happen. And to my editor, Jackie Kaiser, my thanks go beyond words: you shared my vision from the beginning, and your unshakeable faith brought it to light.

To my husband, Peter, my thanks for your support, both technical and emotional, and for your loving belief in me; and to my son, Jacob, thank you for sharing with me your wise and exuberant spirit, and your stories of coyotes, stones and spirits.

Beth Powning
August 1995

CONTENTS

BOUNDARIES

"Our soul is our dream of the other."

GARY SNYDER

BOUNDARIES

The coyotes are newcomers.

Several years ago, they moved into the forests above our farm. They came softly, without preamble, like sand dunes formed by the winds of night.

We encountered them in the slanting light of an August afternoon, when we were taking a short cut home on one of the logging roads back in the hills. They came trotting out of the alders, a pack of seven. They froze, scattered across the road; they stared us dead in the eyes. Their tongues lolled from grinning mouths, and their narrow faces flickered with intelligence honed sharp as lightning. They did not appear to be afraid. In the sudden, reverberant silence, I read in their eyes an indifference so profound that my spirit quailed. They had been moving fast, and they paused only for an instant, considering us rapidly; then they vanished back into the alders, flickering through the striped shadows like fish in shallows. The casual swing of their paws, the calm and instant resumption of their hunt, proclaimed that we were no more, to them, than clouds in the sky.

Our farm lies at the end of a valley.

At night, lying in bed, I feel as if I am in the cabin of a ship; the hills and fields rise around me like dark seas and I feel secure, with the womb-sense of being cradled in a familiar darkness as I pass through the larger darkness of night. To the south of the farm are marshy pastures where hawks hunt on summer mornings; to the west, a road winds down the valley to the Bay of Fundy, like a necklace sparsely beaded with gray barns, white houses. To the north, and the east, fields roll over the steep hills—hayfields, pastures— until they meet the forest, a prickly wall of spruce and fir, the boundary line between wilderness and farm.

It's a threshold, a place I can stand with one foot on spruce needles and the other on timothy grass. The coyotes flicker down through the trees, and gather here, on the edge of our domain, on the edge of theirs. They sit on their haunches, and sing.

They sing in the well of night when I have been asleep for a long time. The sound rises over the thin crickets of midsummer. It is carried on the breeze that fingers our sleeping faces, and pulls me just to the edge of consciousness. It spirals past layer on layer of memory, mingling with dream, and touches the dark place in me that connects, tenuously, with this wild ululation.

I lie, listening, and then I slide out from under the quilt and kneel on the floor with my chin on the windowsill. It's cold on a July night in the Maritimes; the moon has set. I can see the hills, black curves darker than the sky. I can hear the steady, irregular burble of the mint-choked brook.

The wild singing comes again. Sharp, piercing yelps rise, one by one, solitary cries, then all together, a rushed, tremulous babble, a chaos of sound utterly unlike any human music. When it dies away, the dark valley cups the echo of the echo, the cricket-song falters and then resumes a half-tone higher. Other ears than mine are listening.

The chorus rises into the cold air, again and again. I imagine the sharp, wary coyote faces lifted to the sky, eyes half-closed in abandonment to the frenzied yipping. It is not a beautiful song. Unlike the wolf's howl, you can't answer it with a flute. It doesn't thread silver through the night like the call of a thrush, or a loon. Yet when the sound dies, I realize I am as expectant as if I had understood, as if I were waiting for the next message. It is the voice of the wild. It

is direct, raw; it is all that came first.

There is something in me that knows this voice. It is a wisp, impossible to grasp, like the merest sense of the fragment of a dream. Crouched at the windowsill, and beginning to shiver, I'm on a threshold, like the coyotes.

But I choose oblivion, and creep back under the quilt, allowing sleep to wrap me in its muffling layers, to bind me with its spinning surreal images; while the coyotes lower their muzzles, and trot down the ridge as the stars begin to pale in the morning sky.

The Ghosts of Brambly Hollows

They seeped into this corner of the world, the coyotes, following something more than instinct. They came, not with the territorial imperative of migrating birds, but carefully, noses to the ground,

sniffing out new paths.

They knew precisely what they sought, but not where to find it. Thus they came swiftly, making clear choices at every streambed, every fork in the trail, every highway crossed, every town skirted. Traveling, always, towards the familiar, they paused at the grass crushed by a leather boot, the rock spattered with a drop of dog's saliva, and turned away into the ferns, where fox paws had sketched a trail.

Home, for the coyotes, is always the same, only in a new place.

It's different for humans. Home is harder to locate, if you set out to find it.

When my husband, Peter, and I were first married, some twenty years ago, we started our life in the place I had always called home. We lived in a tiny house in the New England village where my family had been stolidly putting down roots for two hundred years. We lived across the street from my grandparents' house, with its verandahs and stone walls, its myrtle beds and giant maples. We kept chickens in a pen; put a sign for McGovern on the front lawn. Every Tuesday night, we crossed the street to the flat-roofed Federal house where the front rooms were library and the librarian lived in the ell. We'd hook our legs around the chair legs, we'd sit at the round tables with their green-shaded lamps, and in the ritual silence, enveloped in the sweet, somnolent smell of books, we read about wilderness adventure in Canada and Alaska. We read about the homesteaders of the 1930s.

In those years, childhood had not yet become a separate realm for me, and yet it was slipping away, its elements becoming hazy, and beloved: the narrow roads lined with stone walls and maple trees, black and white cows drifting across rocky pastures, meetings of the Ladies Aid Society, dusty trucks at the Brooklyn fair. Calves, jam, rhubarb stew. Blackbirds in the marsh. Buckets of wild grapes on porch steps. I remembered those things and watched as farms twenty miles to the south were sold for shopping malls. I saw trees topple. I watched bulldozers knock apart stone walls, flatten barns, level pastures. Cars parked, neon glared, and people, oblivious, licked ice-cream cones over the ghosts of brambly hollows.

It was rushing up on us, the new world. In my town, farmers grew old and cows dwindled in the fields. Clotheslines disappeared. There were no red chickens pecking on driveways. Farms became shells, empty, waiting to be gathered.

Two dreams evolved.

The first was the dream of the wild. In this one, we would pack the necessities for survival in a canoe, we'd paddle far up some northern river, build a cabin, run a trapline. We would live on a lake, cross its ice on snowshoes when we trekked out for supplies, carry our baby in a backpack. It would be a long time before civilization caught up to us. We would take what the earth had to offer, be at the mercy of the frozen lake, and the narrow-eyed predators. We would live on the edge; survival would be dicey.

The second was the dream of the garden. The place of this dream might be south, or west, but in some warm hollow we imagined meadows, a small house, herbs hung from beams, an apple orchard and a Jersey cow. The climate would be benign, and we would take charge of our survival. Honey, potatoes, butter, cabbage; root cellar and cold frame, hives and harrows; we'd propitiate nature, learn her ways.

We wavered back and forth between these concepts, imagining ourselves in furs (heroic), in overalls (humble); but in both dreams the impulse was the same. It was an impulse that was deeper than imagination, sturdier than dream. My grandfather's apple press had fallen silent. The apple trees grew gray with twigs, and the blades of the windmill no longer whirled, creaking, over the barn roof. I loved the rhythms of my childhood. I couldn't bear their extinction.

A moment must come when all the coyotes sense, suddenly, that it is dangerous to remain, imperative to seek new territory.

If humans occasionally obey this instinct, impulses both of memory and survival push us onward.

What is life without brambly hollows and blackbirds?

So we contemplated the colors on a map of North America, chose a

place at random. It was across the border, in Canada; it was far enough north to satisfy parts of the first dream, far enough south to plug in bits of the second. We imagined a life, and then set out to find it.

Searching, driving with maps, we made one hesitant choice and then another, looking for beauty, looking for peace. You might as well say that the winds blew us to this valley.

Northern Night

It was early spring, in New England, when we were finally ready to make our move.

I could feel the season bursting around me, birds flying low trailing bits of yellow grass, green willows softening the river banks, the air sharp with the plangent smells of mud and manure.

We withdrew, day by day, cutting threads, disengaging. We were intent, taut, bursting like the season with the energy of renewal. We had grown into this New England spring, had watched violets opening at the base of lichened stone walls, knew that the bluebirds had returned. On the eve of departure, I realized I would not see what came next. I was abandoning the lilacs three days before they would burst into purple and white clusters. The hot summer would come without me.

We left just before sunrise. My parents stood under the weeping willow that my father had planted when I was born. The tree rose higher than the house, and its boughs hung very still in the hush of dawn. As the truck rolled backward, the headlights isolated my parents as they stood together, waving, with brave smiles. My tears made this last image, which I wanted to be of the utmost clarity, blur and waver.

We turned the corner; my childhood dropped away behind me.

All day long, I felt a peculiar passivity; in the space between the end of one era, and the start of another, I was free for one day to exist in neither. The humming engine, relentlessly carrying us onward, was the final force of all the forces we had set in motion. Like a twist of a kaleidoscope, its momentum would change all the colored pieces, forever.

As we drove north to New Brunswick, the season rolled farther and farther back. The grass grew paler, buds were more tightly furled. Cirrus clouds wisped in a colder sky. Hour after hour I watched as the trees changed, and oaks and hickories were replaced by dark pines, and then fir, and spruce. At dusk, the jagged spears of spruce trees were blackly etched against a yellow light, and when darkness fell, I was shocked to see snow-covered fields revealed in the long sweep of oncoming headlights.

Spring had vanished as completely as if I had dreamt it.

It was very late when we turned onto the final stretch of road. Lights fell from windows, spreading warm yellow squares on the snow; but the houses grew fewer and farther between. We crossed a covered bridge, came to a blue and white store, where one light cast a harsh brilliance over a single gas pump. *You turn left at the store.* We left the highway, ground up a hill on a dirt road. The deep ruts were frozen, and the trailer behind our pick-up truck swerved and jounced, making our headlights sear nightmarishly across alders, snowbanks, gray barns.

Home. The driveway was washed out. We lurched through slush, slid into a snowbank and could go no farther.

We stumbled through knee-deep snow towards the looming bulk of the house. No lights lay in welcoming oblongs; no smoke wavered from the chimney. The house was empty and silent, and as unknown to me as the trees over my head, whose branches rattled on a bitter wind, or the snow that soaked the knees of my jeans, snow I had not seen fall and could hardly accept as real.

Illiterate in the ways of the north, I could not read the messages conveyed by the night air. I saw only blackness, heard only silence. I did not know the new voice of the brook, running in full spate under the snow; I could not judge the relative moisture of the air on my cheek, or see how the stars had shifted over the barn roof.

The house was deadly cold. The mattress was damp. The power had been disconnected, and so we lit a candle in the bedroom and took rugs off the floor and piled them on top of our sleeping bag. One window entirely filled the north wall of the small, slope-ceilinged room. It was uncurtained, and the small flickering star of our candle glistened in runnels of condensation that crept down the black panes. That night, the house was still with the silence of a house that has stood empty through a long winter. I sensed the beginning of the process by which nature claims such houses; frost sparkled on the plaster ceilings, and as we huddled under our rugs we could hear the dry scrabble of mice in the laths.

It took me a long time to fall asleep. I kept picturing my parents standing under the willow tree. In my mind's eye, they had become tiny, wistful people in a place that might not really exist.

I pressed my fists against my chest, curled my body around the ache of loss, as if I might contain it. The house had its own peculiar smell of wood smoke and dead mice. I absorbed it with every breath, as if I slept with a stranger. I felt, suddenly, the utter

strangeness of this place. I wondered if we were equal to the black press of the northern night just beyond the wet glass.

A dream is a dream; but I had stepped into mine.

A SEA OF GRASSES

I remember an afternoon in late August, that first summer. The sky was white. The south wind had crossed the Fundy coast, carrying with it the putrescent tang of salt flats, of seaweed. I stood on a wooden stoop that hung crookedly from the front door. The house was like a ship adrift in a sea of grasses. I watched the timothy tossing in a high wind, their blue-green seed heads sweeping forward in supple waves. All the leaves on the maples clung to their stems, pulled northward by the wind; pale, belly-side up, they furled into tiny cigars. The wind shredded petunias, lifted wood shingles. Swallows sheared sideways. There was a vast rushing summer wind-

song, eternal as the boom of surf.

I stared down the valley, holding my hair away from my face. I wanted to listen easily, to know without considering, to see from a true perspective. But I stood outside every moment. I stood on the stoop as an alien, an immigrant. I did not belong here.

Must one *be long* in order to belong? So it seemed. Nothing had depth, since I had no association with anything. My eyes and my heart skimmed the surface of this world.

On this afternoon, with its opaque sky, I wondered if we had stepped into the wrong dream. The austere barns, empty of cows and horses, the jewelweed growing in blackened hay, the vast and treeless fields, the swallows who circled the house and the barns with absolute supremacy and indifference: none of this could have anything to do with me.

There was no reason to be here other than the idealism that we held before ourselves like a compass. We knew no one, had no connections. I had thought this would not matter. I had believed that if nothing happened in a day except for the sunrise and the V-flight of migrating geese, that if I did little more than harvest vegetables from the garden or bake bread in the wood stove, that should be enough.

This farm on the edge of the wilderness would be a distillation of everything I loved, essence of wildflowers and sky, like a wine whose taste quickens memory.

I thought that to hear the voice of the wild all you had to do was listen.

I stood on the stoop, staring down the valley at the farms I could see across the fields. *What does it look like, what do I see?* I had no framework, only the immigrant's vanished past which perverts the present with nostalgia. I yearned to make this place my own, but it was like trying to learn a language without a dictionary or a friend to translate.

I went back into the house and stood in the doorway of the kitchen.

The room was in passage: it was not yet our own, but it no longer bore the stamp of its previous owners. We had stripped the walls of their obdurate wallpaper, returning them to their starting point of horsehair-reinforced plaster. The floor was strewn with fragments of wallpaper matted into pulp. Wires dangled from the wall where we had ripped out an electric stove. A newly purchased Beaverbrook-Fawcett wood cookstove filled the east end of the room, and white sea-light fell on a Mason jar of goldenrod and steeplebush that I had set on its warming oven. In all the white and restless emptiness, this stove, with its crown of wildflowers, was friendly, welcoming, our first connection.

When you live in the same place for a long time, you don't think about how the things around you are accessible. The morning sky is close and familiar because you've stood in the same spot, morning after morning, and the clouds, the mist, the smell of balsam are inseparable from the smell of sun-warmed shingles, the texture of the door jamb where you place your hand, and the knowledge that the people you love have watched the same sky, from the same place, for generations.

As a child, when I stood on the bank of my uncle Jim's pond, I recalled not only my own adventures there, but my father's, and his parents', and so on and on, back for two hundred years. Each added layer of memory shaped the texture of ponds, trees, old barns, each generation adding the vision of the one that came before, the way an ancient ants' nest builds grain on grain, and sprawls, softly.

Staring into the kitchen, I realized that I would never see this room as I had seen the kitchens of my childhood.

I had deliberately torn away from the dark tangle of family, from deep knowledge of a few square miles, where the past was inseparable from the present. I had left a place that I knew with visceral memory, where the familiar stone wall was alive in the palms of my hands, and my cousins and I played in an attic filled with spinning wheels and hat boxes. Here, the first roots were put down by me.

Homesickness. The child's anguish, alone in a strange bed, is a searing ache; for the exile, the immigrant, the ache is pervasive, a sense of never belonging, of being someone to whom everyone is polite,

27

of having no intuitive knowledge of place, no connecting stories. The outsider lives in the same place as everyone else, walks side by side, eyes seeing the same things differently.

Home. You have to weave it, thread by thread.

I took a sponge and soaked the last clinging bits of wallpaper. I wanted to purge the house of anything that held someone else's history. I wanted it to be utterly empty.

Wind whished through the patched, buckled mesh of the screen door. A ravel of flypaper began to swing randomly, and I could smell wet plaster, damp wallpaper, the raw scent of old dreams, dissolving.

As I worked, the only sound in the room was the dry scratch of my scraper across the damp plaster. Puritanically, we had no radio. The phone would not ring; although we could call out, no one could call in. Outside, the wind roared in the old maples and the white phlox by the south door tossed and thrashed helplessly. I could hear the slap and crack of tea-towels on the line, and the persistent, chirring rasp of crickets. From far away came the crying of birds as they soared on updrafts and shot sideways on slipstreams, diving, dancing in the warm, rocketing air.

The house, like a shell, amplified the sounds of wind and crickets and birds. I listened to the August afternoon, hearing a language I could not speak, a language spoken and sung by creatures who did not care whether they were heard, or understood.

FRONTIERS

A frontier is a margin; it's the place between long-settled territory and the land still to be conquered. It is like the front, in a battle. It's where there's a clash of wills.

We lived on the edge of what we thought was wilderness. *There's nothing but forest,* we were pleased to tell people, *from our farm all the way to the ocean.* But as we drove around the back roads in our pick-up truck, we came across scenes of desolation, places of defeat.

We took our binoculars, seeking hawks, moose, great blue herons; but what drew us, as we roamed the back roads, were the abandoned farms. They attracted us the way you cannot help hearing your own language spoken in a foreign country. They stood in overgrown meadows, sun-warmed pockets that were welcoming after miles of dark trees. A house might stand there, its roof buckled, its doors and windows hanging crookedly. In the grass we'd find rusted buckets without bottoms, pieces of bone china. Stunted perennials survived, spreading under the alders; yellow day lilies, pink roses, columbine. If there was a solitary maple left in what had been the yard, it would be half-dead, bone-white branches scattered at its base. Lilac bushes had trunks thick as my leg, twisted like cables.

Just above our valley, an entire community had vanished within living memory. Our oldest neighbor went up there one day with a stack of shingles. She'd painted names on them; "the McFarlane Place," "Cheese Factory," "School." She nailed them to trees in the forest where once there had been clearings, where all these buildings had stood square-sided and strong, cedar shingles bright in the sunshine of her memory. She could not bear that there was nothing to mark their passing. The shingles lasted for several years, fading, slipping sideways, falling one by one.

The old Lisson place was a mile east of our farm, on a hill that rose beyond the hardwood ridge. The house stood bleakly, exposed to all the winds at the very top of the knoll. Its windows were black holes. Whole sections of its wood-shingled roof had collapsed. We went inside, picking our way carefully across the sagging floor. From the empty windows, you could see nothing for fifty miles but blue hills, trees and sky. Plaster crunched underfoot; over our heads, rafters striped the blue sky. The house was no more than a frame, a moldering cage containing a rubble of broken glass, mattress stuffing, plaster, dusty laths, chipped enamel pitchers, wet magazines, a dog skull pierced by a bullet hole.

Outside in the harsh light, I noticed a well-trodden trail winding through the grass. Porcupines had claimed the cellar.

They had failed, these people.

I heard the cold whishing of the wind in the spruce trees. It makes the same sound in summer as in winter, a remote sound that comes from high overhead. I saw the wispy grass ripple in the overgrown meadow.

I stepped down from what had been the back door and I imagined the woman who might have stood there, listening to the wind, or watching snow swirl out of a black night. I imagined her staring hopelessly into the darkness and longing for her spring-green Irish fields. I could hear the emptiness with her ears.

We stood there, my husband and I, talking about what a crazy place it had been to build a house, exposed to fifty unbroken miles of the wind's momentum. Two more winters, and the house would be down. After a while, you'd never know it had been here at all. In this way we mocked their vision, these vanished people, and avoided making any comparison to ourselves.

There are two sides to a battle, and two kinds of desolation. The vanquished farms lay basking in the summer sun, broken glass glittering in the weeds with a kind of sentinel warning; their cold cellars smelled of exhaustion, of poor choices, and bad luck.

But the places humans had vanquished were infinitely more desolate.

We were driving with the windows open. Cool, resinous air breathed from the dark woods and white bunchberries tumbled over banks beside the road.

We turned a corner and saw a wasteland.

Bleeding stumps and sawdust and dismembered branches and uprooted violets. Plastic oil containers. Pop cans. Pools of chainsaw oil. Geometric tire tracks. A gray rack and ruin of maimed and tortured trees as profane as the flensed remains of the great whales. Not a tree left standing; the silver purl of a tiny stream wending its way through the torn land. No birds, no animals. Blue sky bending

over a new desert. No sound of wind; there was nothing left to
catch it.

By the roadside, I noticed a collection of cigarette butts, chip bags,
Styrofoam, glass bottles: someone seemed to have gathered it
together, like an offering for the gods.

THE MYSTERY BEHIND THE SNOW

We thought we knew what we wanted, when we dreamed our life.
Farm, wilderness, side by side. The tamed, the wild. We wanted to
hold the earth in our hands and make it work for us; we wanted to
know, first-hand, the power that moves the stars.

When you live in the constant presence of what isn't tame, and you
expect the unknown—a moose trotting down the driveway at dusk,
a fox in the goldenrod, a bear with her cubs browsing at the edge of
the field—you discover the complexity of your own place in
creation. You feel like someone on the outside, looking in. A
coyote's eyes can annihilate.

We lived through our first winter. I felt the weight and immensity,
the white obliterating power of the north. I felt its violence, its
mystery, like a yeti hovering beyond the veils of snow I could
glimpse but never quite see. I understood that the desire to control
comes from a well of frustration and fear; it is easier to cut down
the forest and silence the bloody wind than it is to seek the mystery
behind the snow.

And I began to understand why people asked us with such amazement why young folks like ourselves had come *here*.

In February, the first winter, I pressed my nose to the glass of the living-room window and looked out. I could see dense smoke pouring from a chimney, rising over Balm of Gilead trees; it came from the house of an eighty-year-old man who walked the roads with an axe, collecting green alder for his stove. I could see the other solitary bachelor's farm across the meadow; his barn was collapsing, segments crumbling every few months, timbers buckling, a pall of ancient hayseed rising into the silent air.

In winter, when I went walking, the only sound was the croak of a raven and the crunching of my snowshoes; white snow, white sky, white smoke. Sometimes I felt like a piece of seed fluff, cut loose, drifting aimlessly through time.

SMALL TRUTHS

Gradually, very gradually, this valley became my home.

I had to bury the ache of memory and nostalgia that began the first night we slept in this house. I had to learn to see. I had to look and listen closely, to pay attention, in order to blend with the shadows. It was like being a child again, reawakening perception. Connection starts from the inside.

I learned small truths, and collected them, like a harvest. *Black frost, so cold the fields smoke. Put the logs flat-side down. Crickets play dead. Cumulus clouds over fireweed; thunder in August. Plant beans when the wild cherries*

35

blossom. Wool mittens inside leather ones. Frozen wood splits clean. Dust on the goldenrod, the plovers are massing.

I learned that summer air is sharp, rather than drowsy. There are chokecherries, not Concord grapes. No stone walls, but stone cairns, instead. And emptiness became space; silence became peace. Desolation is a state of mind. I no longer stare, frightened, into the night.

We planted bushes at the corners of the house, added porches and windows, tore down walls. We made gardens and lawns. We planted red pines along the fields, built a pond, cut alders. We fenced pastures and built treehouses and hung swings and splashed in puddles with a child whose eyes rested on this valley first, and for whom these hills would be, easily, home.

It takes a long time for roots to grow. For me, twenty years passed before I suddenly realized that this place had finally become home.

It became my home when I knew, absolutely and without looking, that the wind would tug loose the fireweed's seed fluff in the last week of August; when I knew where to find the fiddleheads, and could tell by the sound of the brook when they would be ready; when I could watch spindrifts of snow ghosting across the fields and remember dew-hung spider webs on a June morning, like a reality behind reality. It is the small events of the natural world, the return of the swallows, the leaping gray waters of the spring brooks, that comfort me with a kind of transcendent familiarity, an ancient re-awakening. Freshets are freshets anywhere on the planet. The swallows soar to this valley from the skies of Central America. The moon shines over the Sahara, and rain is rain.

But these events can no longer be taken for granted.

I came here because in the countryside of my childhood, brooks were vanishing under parking lots. The night sky was no longer black, and arc lights obscured the stars. Swallows flew over a paved marsh, searching for their nesting sites. Cities stretched over so much territory, with such presumptuous energy, that no one remembered the forests that had once grown there, just as we forget vanquished civilizations.

It's only now that I begin to understand the instinct that drove me to abandon my human connections, to flee the invading bulldozers.

Memory.

I am three years old, and down the road, Maisie Polom is waving a stick at her cows, calling each one by name. Rhode Island Reds are scratching up her flower beds. Sheets snapple on an east wind.

Survival.

I'm five years old, and I know about the sacredness of bluets, and the primacy of trees, the world that came first.

And yet, seek as I might, there are boundaries I can't cross. I'm standing in the field, hand shading my eyes. I hear the garbled honking of autumn geese, and they pass over me, so close that I can hear the rush of air under their great wings. I watch them become a wishing-bone in the sky, vanishing between the blue hills. Leaves fall and skitter over the close-cropped grass. Crickets chirr.

Boundaries: between the geese and me, between the crickets and me. Yet the longer I listen, the more I hear.

I hear wind in the grass. I hear water, splashing over rocks. I hear the creak of tree bole, and the hollow rapping of a woodpecker. I hear pine needles, whispering.

The heart of the wild eludes me.

Yet I come close to it.

It turns in my own heart, like a key that unlocks wonder, and reverence.

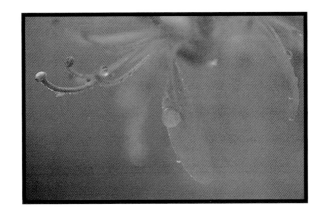

BOUNDARIES

GARDENS

"What shall I learn of beans, or beans of me?"
HENRY DAVID THOREAU

". . . the mind is trying to find its place within
the land, to discover a way to dispel its own
sense of estrangement."
BARRY LOPEZ

There were no gardens when we arrived. The house stood alone, surrounded by fields. When we looked out the windows, our eyes traveled with the rippling grass all the way up to the forest.

I felt exposed under so much sky. I wanted something between me and the dark trees.

Of the two dreams, farm and wilderness, I leaned towards the first. Nasturtiums came before trilliums. I needed to frame the sky before I could love its serenity.

So I took a piece of the field nearest to the house and converted its wild tangle into a garden. Over the years, I pushed back the fields by making perennial beds, digging a kitchen garden by the back door, planting daffodils under the maples. I put in raspberries, a double-dug strawberry bed, lilac bushes. I started lilies and roses and planted clematis on the garden fence.

I made a zone of domesticity, a place where I could kneel quietly in a sheltered place, the sun hot on my shoulders, my hands in the soil, and begin to make my acquaintance with this piece of earth.

Although I plant the potatoes in a different bed each year, or try a new kind of chard, I take the same journey, I repeat the same rhythms, over and over again, until I feel like the swallows who return to the same nests summer after summer and make new babies.

This will be the twenty-fifth summer I have planted a vegetable garden on this piece of ground, and still I go out in the morning and stand on the path, squinting against the warm wind, worrying about whether the seeds will sprout. I have tamped them into the soil and they lie hidden under the marks of the rake tines that line the soil like dark zippers. I stare anxiously at all the hopeful stakes, the reminders that I have set for myself so I will know, when they sprout, the difference between Green Arrow and Laxton's Progress peas. This is the stage between vision and truth, when I suddenly doubt my faith. I kneel and furtively uproot a seed with my finger to see if it has put forth its slim green tail, to see if, like a baby bird, the cotyledon has cracked its shell.

This is an underground event. Like the coyote's song, it excludes me; it's a boundary I can't cross. This is one of the great mysteries, a dance that has gone on since life began. Nature chooses the moment of birth. There's nothing I can do if the seeds rot in cold soil, if a heavy rain washes them out of the ground, or if no rain comes and it snows, instead. There's nothing to do but wait.

When the beans come arching through the soil like green staples, the carrots sprout in grassy lines, and the nasturtiums unfold their lily-pad leaves, I'm relieved, filled with the same excitement every year. My offering has been accepted, and now I'm caught up in a partnership with the soil and the sky. It is a bargain of sorts; there will be tests, and trials. And yet there will be no holding my part-ners to account, and the tiny plants that I consider "mine" will be subject to the same cold nights and late frosts and summer wind storms as the vigorous thistles, the plantain, the wood sorrel, and the violets.

It's hard to imagine anything but warm sun and gentle rain; there's such stretching, such striving. It's like seeing my own life in micro-cosm, or my child's. I can't bear the possibility of a brutal end to this intense growth. I guard against the cutworms that could drain the sap from a cabbage; I spread blankets over the beans so they

GARDENS

won't be blackened by frost.

Each garden reaches its moment of perfection. Here, it happens in late June, when tiny pea pods overlap on the vines and the corn sprouts hold beads of water trembling in their chaliced leaves. The soil is rich as chocolate, and light glows in the oakleaf lettuce like sun through a rabbit's ear.

Every year at this time, I think that I am going to grow my best garden yet. This will be the summer when the days are hot enough to ripen tomatoes, the summer when the full moon in June will come on a cloudy night, the year when all the carrots will grow long, straight, crisp, and sweet.

Making a garden is like creating a home. This is the day you finally move in. There are no scars, no scratches on the walls, and you stand in the ordered, fresh-smelling rooms and harbor the illusion that the hard work is now over and that all you have to do is keep the house as perfect, as filled with promise as it is at this moment.

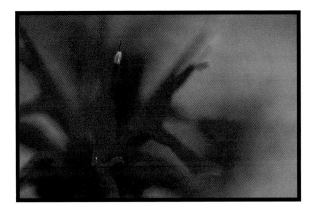

I am thinking only about nurturing these young plants. I am not contemplating the harvest. I don't even think about eating them. I simply watch with amazement as they send down their roots and reach for the light with the intensity of migrating birds. I feel that all will be well, during this brief period of the garden's perfection; I am calm with the conviction that here, at least, is one place where I have some influence, some control. I am the guardian of these plants. I am the steward of this kingdom.

Six o'clock on a June morning; sun slants in hazy bands across the garden. In the raised beds, shadows double the blue-green onions and garlic. The wood-chip paths are dark with dew. A cat crouches on the wooden fence, intent upon sharpening her claws. A pink mist of sweet-smelling flowers cloaks the honeysuckle, and spider webs tremble in the grass. It is a moment of pure stillness, as if the bachelor's buttons and cauliflower and lovage, like horses dreaming in ground mist, have been asleep and are now touched awake by the first rays of the imperious sun.

I take my hoe. It is so easy to nick the shallow-rooted weeds from their tenuous holds; to work my fingers between sturdy onions; to pull the straw up around cabbages, like tucking blankets around a child.

For a brief time, the garden is like my own kitchen, whose geraniums and cooling bread reveal my life; for a while, the garden grows just as I imagined it would, just the way I sketched it on paper, last February. I stand between its ordered rows and look out over the fields where clumps of wild flag iris and purple avens make blue pools in the grass along the brook. A fence separates the garden from this world of tossing grasses and rampant, uncontrolled growth, and helps foster the illusion that the garden, like my kitchen, is part of me.

The Tapestry of Summer

And so it is, for a while.

Quickly, though, it passes this quiet stage and moves on to a startling urgency of growth, as urgent as the low-flying swallows who sweep and wheel, ceaselessly hunting insects for their babies in the woodshed, readying them for the autumn flight to Costa Rica.

Thistles with roots like parsnips erupt through the straw in the cabbage bed. Mint creeps slyly amongst the broccoli. My fingers fly like a typist's around the corn stalks, scrabbling away weeds which spring up nightly. Suddenly the radishes are woody and worm-riddled, and their tops have borne flowers and gone to seed. The thick-leafed Bloomsdale spinach passes beyond the dark succulence of its first growth and begins to yellow, and then to bolt. The potatoes need hilling; orange beetle larvae cover the undersides of their leaves. Peas burst like budding breasts against their slim packets, and I thin the carrots in hurried handfuls.

Like swallows, like buttercups and hawkweed and daisies, vegetables follow the imperatives of this valley as precisely as the mathematical certitude of sun and stars. One thousand feet above the sea that is only a few miles away, there is little real heat, and yet light still pales the evening sky at eleven, and rises in the east at five. Each day, long as it is, must be dense with growth, for the August moon will bring the killing frost.

The summer is like the separate beauty of each flower, its piercing loveliness so fleeting that it is gone almost before I have grasped its wonder. All its stages wash past, wave upon wave, wild strawberries engulfed by seas of pink clover, and then daisies and red-top grass, and finally crickets, goldenrod, and fireweed. The first growth, tender as new skin in its early opening, is replaced by thick leaves, a dark sturdiness of growth that rises, uncheckable. Weeds appear, only to be ignored, because it is time, now, to reap a harvest from this bounty, to take what is offered quickly, for I have only one chance, and winter is as inevitable as this majestic fertility.

Late July, early August; the garden pressures me with its heedless and chaotic production. Keeping up with it is like trying to prepare dinner with guests in the kitchen, children underfoot, the phone ringing, and unexpected visitors pulling into the driveway and honking their horn.

On the back porch, I sit with baskets and bowls between my feet, and pinch the sealed edges of a long, green pod. My thumb pulls

53

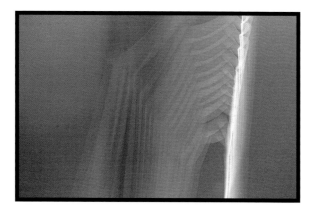

out five, six, seven peas. One bowl is filled with empty pods, for the chickens; the other holds peas which I scoop, with both hands, like pearls.

Or I am in the kitchen; through the window, the long grasses run before the wind, and on the table are mounds of green beans. Water is boiling on the stove; steam makes the lids dance and rattle. My knife flashes, chops, and my hands follow each other fluidly through familiar choreography. In the garden, the onion tops have collapsed in a soft tangle. It seems only yesterday that I planted the tiny sets. There is a peculiar satisfaction in the swiftness with which I pluck the onions from the soil and lay them in golden ranks to cure. Twist and pull the corn ears, tuck them under my arm. Shuck them in the garden and throw the husks to the horses.

As the light becomes lower and richer, I feel a gathering sense of fulfillment, and loss.

It happens too fast. Yet in this speed, this urgency that inhibits

reflection, in the busy-ness of living, in the demands of vegetable growing, I am absorbed by the life of this particular soil, this particular air, and this particular light. I become a thread in the tapestry of summer, even as I am torn by the desire to stand aside, the need to arrest this tumbling beauty, to hold it in my hands.

The garden is no longer part of me; I have become part of it.

THE MIRACLE OF THE SEEDS

Then, like a well-lived life, comes the quiet.

I pull up plants that have finished their cycle. Into the wheelbarrow I toss bolted lettuce, bush beans whose leaves are brown and crunchy, and exhausted zucchini.

Russian sunflowers stand over these patches of empty earth, and

GARDENS

their enormous heads hang lower, day by day. Blue jays, like brilliant brooches, pin themselves to the pendulous heads and busy themselves with the seeds. They call to one another, plaintively. Their cries are clear, and seem to echo in the autumn air, and then I realize that the swallows have disappeared. The barns seem abandoned, without their swift commanding swoops through doors, under eaves. There's a strangely desolate calm.

The sweet pulse of crickets rises around me, wherever I stand. As the nights grow colder, the chorus fades until only a few survivors sing, separately, in the dying grass.

There is a different kind of peace in the garden, now. It is not the serenity born of potency, and affirmation, but the quiet of fulfillment, and endings.

I have saved the last phase of these plants, their final statement. Garlic hangs in a braid; paper-skinned onions fill bushel baskets. The carrots lie side by side in damp peat moss in the root cellar, and stacks of blueberry crates hold Yukon Golds and Red Pontiacs. In the garden, only husks remain.

Leaves, on the corn stalks, are white and brittle as snakeskins, and have dried in the fluted forms of their green growing. The earth, its fertility transferred, lies sprawled, tossed, the potato furrows littered with hay. A few pea pods swing stiffly on brittle vines, their skins puckery as parchment. On the manure pile, the sunflowers fall sideways, and the once relentless lambs'-quarters are pale and limp.

Even in these husks, the mystery remains. It is the miracle of the seeds, the same mystery glimpsed in the blush of new life. It is the mystery that checks the northward voyage of the sun, and turns it back again. It is the mystery that travels in black river water twisting under moonlight.

At the end of the season, my garden plan is all but forgotten, and my illusion of stewardship long gone. Instead, like another harvest, there is another year's memory of the voyage I have taken, swept, like a leaf, away from my own small visions and into the vast, potent current of regeneration.

Autumn is like a long, deep breath drawn after some endeavor of great intensity.

Nasturtium leaves rot, quietly, into the soft mold between the raspberry canes.

In the end is the beginning.

In the garden is the whole universe.

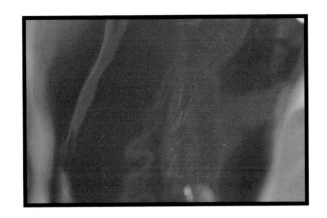

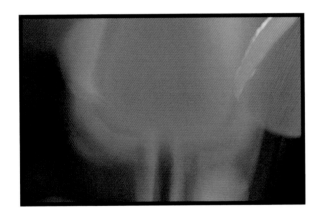

GARDENS

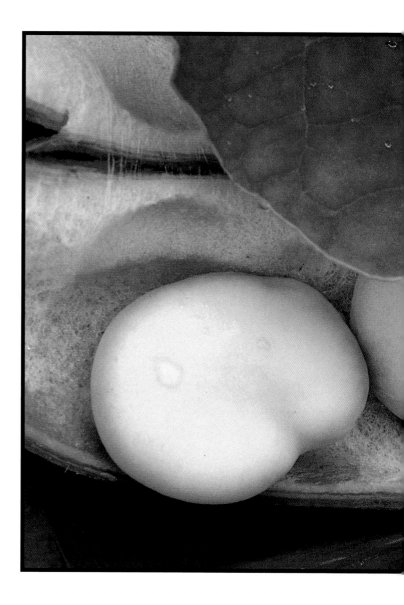

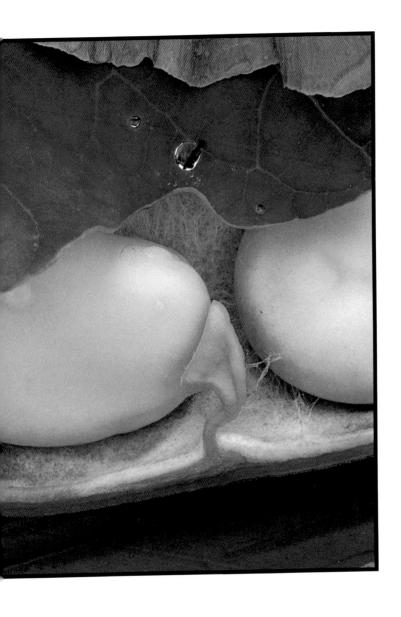

FIELDS

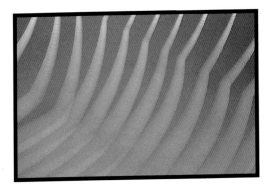

". . . the farm is headed for the woods. The wild is already veined in it everywhere, its thriving."

WENDELL BERRY

FIELDS

The farther I walk into a field, the smaller I feel. All around me, insects trill; bobolinks fly low, scolding, or warning. It is a domestic place, a neat rectangle bordered by fences, but its heart is wild.

In the farming valley of my childhood, fields were small and bordered by stone walls. They were like someone's back yard: *Ernie's pasture, Stone's cornfields, the Lewis meadow*. You did not go into them without circumspection. No one would have minded very much if they had found a small girl slipping between the rustling rows of corn; but these fields, wrested from the inhospitable New England soil, were places of purpose, of human dominion, and the will of the farmer brooded over them, keeping outsiders from crossing their borders.

In early spring, when barn roofs shone in the sun and catkins dangled from willows, the farmers began to work the fields. The monotonous diesel-drone of tractors rose all around our house along with the quarreling of nesting birds and the rushing of spring run-off. Manure spat from battered green spreaders and fell like rich rain on the winter rye. Then the plowing began, the sharp smell of earth edged the air, and the fields turned into patches of brown corduroy.

Around plowing time, the neighbor's cows crossed the road and went up into the summer pastures. Dogs nipped at the stragglers, and from our house I could hear the hoarse shouts of men, the thwack of stick against hide. The cows galloped up the lane in a heaving, jouncing jumble of spring freedom, eyes wide with whites showing and necks outstretched as if reaching for the plaintive moos that had escaped them.

For the rest of the summer, the fields were occupied. Some were

neatly striped, like gardens, with row upon row of silage corn. Others were fenced with creosoted timbers and heavy wire and were grazed close as mowed lawns by massive Holsteins. Hayfields, filled from wall to wall with dancing spears of timothy, were untouched by cultivators, left alone to ripple and swish in the summer winds.

All spring, all summer, my brother and I respected the fields. We knew that we would leave tell-tale trails if we walked through the timothy, that our feet would crack the sprouts of corn, or that if we went into the pastures, the cows would chase our dog and come thundering upon us with lowered heads and sharp hooves.

So we kept to the walls, or bicycled the shady roads. We followed farm lanes to ponds where snapping turtles lurked under lily pads. We walked on pine needles in the state forest, and fished in brooks the color of root beer.

But in the fall, the fields, like the light, changed.

When the harvest was over, and the cows had gone back down to
the barnyard, the will of the farmer was lifted. Corn was in the silos.
Grass had been baled and was stacked in the mow. The cows wore
layers of fat under their coarse white hair. Now we could go into
the fields with impunity. Leftover corn stalks were like miniature
banyan trees, with thick roots, and we hurled them at each other.
They flew high, heavy-ended, spinning against the red evening sky.
We ran down hills, arms flailing for balance as our feet raced to
keep up with our bodies. And in the pastures, gates stood open. We
sat cross-legged on earth worn bare by hooves, and brushed gone-to-
seed thistle heads, soft as our father's shaving brush, against our
cheeks, and then pinched them, sending a thousand seeds drifting to
their destiny.

I loved the fields when their purpose had been served. They seemed
to me to have been released, like an animal that has been untethered
and allowed to roam. I knew the farmers were not paying attention,
that I could wander at my leisure. I could leave the roads that my

feet knew so well; I could climb over the walls and abandon the lane that always led to the same place.

I left my bicycle in a ditch at the side of the road, and as I climbed farther and farther up a hill, the smaller and less my own it seemed. I walked into the very center of a field that had been alien territory all summer. The mild autumn air smelled of leaves and wild grapes. I lay on my back and stretched out my arms.

And as I watched the clouds sailing as if to some destination, I felt myself slipping into the cricketing warmth. The field pulsed with its own rhythm. Crickets rasped, weed seeds fell, ants scurried amongst roots, spiders spun webs, hawks hovered, mice made burrows in dry grass, and deep, deep, the waters of the earth pulsed like a heartbeat I could not hear, but imagined.

Fragile as a Dream

The first time Peter and I saw our farm in New Brunswick, it was the time of wild cherry blossoms. Fragile pink flowers tossed restlessly among dark spruce trees in the hedgerows.

The farm was vacant. House and barns were surrounded by empty fields.

The landscape of my childhood had been overhung by trees. Fields were tucked in valleys or folded between rivers, and they were rimmed with heavy-limbed oaks; everywhere, the sky was framed with a sheltering frieze. But here, on this northern farm, the skies were vast, unbound, sweeping over the swells and hollows of the earth; light and space held dominion, and all things beneath, house, barns, brooks, seemed exposed and diminished. Winds could surge, unchecked, ripping leaves from trees, snatching the cries of birds from their beaks. These hills had once been forested with beech, birch and maple, trees whose branches had subdued autumn gales with a murmurous roar, or cast blue lace-shadow over snow. But humans had uprooted them, and now there was nothing but grass and sky. The farm, surrounded by its swells of treeless land, drifted in space.

That first summer, all the pasture gates stood open, as if cows, dogs, and horses had departed through them. The fields brooded, wild, abandoned, their grasses carrying the wind in sudden stirrings. Brooks rippled down from the hills, twisting through the meadows like silver-blue snakes, and ravens beat from the west, sending harsh cries into the silence like proclamations or warnings.

I felt a sense of recent departure. The muddy farm lanes were patterned with tire treads. Tools hung from spikes on the barn walls— chains, hauling dogs, horse collars. Peaveys and crowbars leaned in corners, just as they had been set down. Last summer's final hay bale waited in the machine to be the first to drop, this year. Everywhere there were signs of interrupted work; of sweat, and necessity.

The land still held the influence of fertilizer, and seed; fields of timothy waved in unbroken seas of tiny blue cigar-heads. It had been a good farm: *best land around*, people told us. But here and there, a fence post rotted at the soil line, tipped forward, and pulled the barbed wire with it. The oat field in the southeast corner had been plowed last fall, and all summer its furrows lay exposed, unharrowed, unseeded, sprouting weeds. In the vacant pastures, feathery red top grew, and then goldenrod, and finally thistles that burst into white seed. There were no cows; the gates stayed open.

The empty barns were dry, silent, their windows blind with dust. Fuzzy light touched gallant names scrolled over the stalls: Prince, King. Dried manure caked the floorboards where cows had stood, their necks rubbing the wooden stanchions smooth as butter. Bits of baling twine wisped from latches; doors creaked on their hinges. Swallows swooped low through the open doors, trailing pieces of grass, making the barns their own.

The fields began at the very foundations of the barns. They swept up to the ridge of the hill, cresting in a ragged row of mountain ash and yellow birch. All along this dividing line were cairns of fist-sized rocks, sprawling piles of countless stones tossed on countless mornings, pried endlessly from furrow upon furrow, year after year, with persistence beyond imagining.

Only a few months ago, there had been sixty cows bawling in the west pasture. There had been sheep, pressed together, trotting in frantic, jouncing spurts across the upper meadows. Belgian horses had grazed, patiently, behind the barns.

Now the ravens flew low, emboldened by the quiet.

The farm was as fragile as a dream.

As the months of summer drifted past, one into the next, the forest began its inevitable return. Alders spread, unchecked. Birds dropped mustard seed in the timothy. Spruce trees sprouted in pastures. Wild cherry pits cracked and sent roots into the bank over the brook. The earth's rhythm, briefly interrupted, resumed.

Everywhere there were signs of animals: raccoon prints starring the mud around a puddle, the cloven hooves of deer scuffing the drive-way. At the very top of the fields, high up where the forests start, blueberry bushes swept like skirts out from under the spruce trees. Here I found the steaming, rank scat of bear and saw how a heavy paw had mauled an ant hill.

In a back field, a fox had made a den in the side of the hill, unpro-tected by bush or tree. Like the ravens, she seemed to know that no tractor would disturb her. I hid upwind in a clump of firs and watched the fox cubs wrestle in the wild strawberries, while the mother fox sat on her haunches, half-lifting a paw, assessing the wind-borne dangers with cold eyes and uplifted ears. Hidden, in the trees, I heard the dropping call of a white-throated sparrow and smelled the wintry, frozen-fern spice of the forest.

Spying on the foxes, interrupting the bear's peaceful feast, I realized how absurd it was to call these fields mine; my hands had never picked a single rock, nor thrown seed, nor driven a post. The fields

were the domain of the bears, the raccoons, and the foxes; they lived
in the dreams and memories of the humans whose forebears had
created them and who had maintained them until now. I was a
stranger.

Yet an uneasy truth fingered my heart like the ripple of wind in the
grasses.

I recalled the overgrown fields around the crumbling cellar holes,
back in the hills. I thought of the earth's tangent, the power of wind
and rain, of seed and rock, the endless blind persistence of regeneration; and then I remembered the generations of immigrants who
had struggled to control and resist the earth, season after season for
a hundred years.

Fields do not exist without human stewardship.

Where did my loyalties lie: with the vanished humans, or the browsing bears?

That summer, the windows of the house were held open by broken pieces of lath, and the ceaseless susurration of the grasses was like the sound of pebbles washed by surf. It was a murmuring that I felt I should listen to, but did not, fully; a sound understood by the heart, but not by the mind.

OF CONTOUR AND HOLLOW

Fields are square, and marked by posts and fences. They are bits of the planet brought to heel, remnants of vanquished forests. Yet within their human geometry, life cycles as complex and remote as the stars follow their course, and patterns more delicate than any human imagining turn, and tremble: the eyes of a butterfly, the iridescent scales of a million grasshoppers' wings.

Fields represent truce, an accommodation of impulses. Perhaps it is thus that they attract us, and then make us feel insignificant. I quickly grew to love the fields. When I walked into them, early on a summer morning, and then turned and looked back at the farm, it was as if I were looking out the window of an airplane at a toy world. The farm fell away, became small and insubstantial; other people, still sleeping or making breakfast, had nothing to do with this world of wildflowers, pink clouds dappling a cool sky, sun trembling in dew, and the waking calls of birds.

The fields beckoned to me, always. Whenever I rested on my shovel, or set down my hammer, I saw the bright swells of waving grass, imperturbably marking the summer's rhythm. The whish of wind, the chuckling of water, the single piercing cry of a bird came from another place, yet one that was close by. The fields and their hidden life followed their own course, whether or not I attended.

It wasn't until the first week in August that Peter and I got around to making hay. By then, ferns in the hedgerows were shifting from green to tigery yellow, and under the willows by the brook fireweed ran rampant. The timothy had flowered, the cigar-heads now soft with seed. Our neighbor nodded, watching our preparations, his eyes lightening with approval and relief. *Late, yes, but still some good in it.*

A rusty red Massey-Harris tractor came with the farm. One morning, as soon as the dew was dry on the grass, Peter began mowing. The cutter bar clattered, its knife blades clicking. It dropped to the ground and was lost under the tall grass. Then the tractor went forward, and the grass trembled and fell backward in silky green swathes all up the hill, and around and around. The tossing tapestry fell, and fell, rectangle within rectangle, until the last waving strip tumbled down, and then all the diverse criss-cross of stems lay neat and culled, arranged, and still.

The next day, after the hay had been raked, I walked along the swathes of freshly-cut grass, tossing the sweet-smelling tangle with a hay fork. All around me the crickets sang freely, as if the tall grass had muffled their song and they celebrated its absence. Swallows dove and wheeled, feasting on hapless insects. I watched the tractor crawl forward, and the baler lick up the swathes. Green cubes dropped, bounced, until the whole field was studded with square packages. Friends were there, that afternoon, and we ranged across the field, standing with hands gripping the hairy binder twine, waiting to sling our bale onto the truck or the hay wagon. Lift and throw, over and over, my arms scratched, sweat in my eyes; the field behind me, as I moved up the hill, was left bare, all the beauty of the earth's form revealed in clean sweeps of contour and hollow.

We hayed for days, until the mows were piled to the roofs, and broken bales filled the aisles, slippery underfoot, springy with recent life.

As the week went by, the landscape changed. From the upstairs windows, I leaned out and saw a pattern, the original plan of the farm.

The wildness was gone. Suddenly, it was easy to stride across the fields, and the farm seemed tidy, bore the illusion of prosperity; the fields were like mowed lawns, running all the way up to the woods.

At night, the sound of the crickets intensified. Thousands and thousands of crickets, their black bodies sleek, their high, hinged legs playing the sweet cadence of autumn; they hopped in the stubble, teemed in the open air, burrowed into the apples that dropped from the trees in the old orchard at the edge of the woods.

Spiders, deprived of their grasses, cast webs on the ground, like diaphanous white scarves.

The Night's Poetry

In late August, I went out after dark. On the air was the spice of decay, the breath of cold water. I wore a jacket, balled my hands in

FIELDS

my pockets. My feet swung easily over the shorn field, and I walked
up the hill in the darkness. The crickets were no longer a chorus,
but called singly, vanishing one by one, as inevitably as falling leaves.

The fields had come into my realm, now, and I remembered them as
places of sweat, of diesel fumes; I remembered them through the
focus of will and determination. They had given me the satisfaction
of harvest. I held their grasses in my barn.

I sat in the middle of the biggest field, and looked down on the valley. All along the road, houses sent their unchanging lights into the
darkness. I knew that inside, the windows mirrored the rooms, and
turned back the rustle of leaf on air, the cold running of waters,
the sharp glitter of the stars.

I looked up at the night sky. High over the tiny lights of our valley,
long shafts of green and white and pink glowed, increased in intensity, faded.

Northern lights, the aurora borealis. I fell onto my back so that I could see all corners of the sky at once, for the ghostly, evanescent shafts shifted endlessly, one melting into the next. Watching them was like trying to recall a dream and catching only a fleeting thread of memory.

The crickets continued their silvery trilling, the brooks trickled quietly, and the galactic event went on and on, as cold, majestic, and contained as hawks riding the wind, as coyotes barking under the moon.

I lay, alone, in the hayfield, my arms out-flung and my palms open. Pure science, the interstellar encounter between atoms and magnetic field lines became, for me, a divine dance, the night's poetry.

Against the eerie, fluxing, greenish-pink rays stood the black spires of the spruce trees along the ridge. And I thought of our sweat on these fields, of our barn filled with hay, and of how year after year until death we'd make hay and still the grass would come back, still the seedlings would sprout, still the aurora borealis would pulse in vast unconcern across the illimitable skies.

As the show played on far overhead, the northern lights raying across the Milky Way, over misty nebulae and diminishing eons of stars, I scrambled to my feet. I needed a human hand, a cup of tea. Awed by infinity, touched by ecstasy—even so, I suddenly needed small, steady lights that sliced across bushes and barns.

I strode down through the fields. I felt my awe diminishing, and a smaller, more familiar elation replacing it, as I felt the sweet soil of the earth, solid under the soles of my rubber boots.

T R E E S

"Trees . . . seem to me the best,
most revealing messengers to us from all nature,
the nearest its heart."

JOHN FOWLES

TREES

The woods of my childhood were as familiar to me as the honey-suckle bush by the back door, or the egg-shaped spot on the stove where the enamel was chipped. Like the faces of my parents, the trees that netted the rising sun just before its rays struck the wall of my bedroom had always been there, and I thought they would always remain.

It was a small wood, not a forest, merely a few acres of trees bordered on all sides by pasture and field. But to a child, it was without bounds, as endless as time or the night sky. My father had mown a swathe through the trees with his Farmall Cub tractor; crickets teemed in the warm grass, and barberry bushes flashed their red berries under a tangle of wild roses. I could follow this path through the woods, the singing of unseen birds in the cool, leaf-dancing light and shadow on either side, until I came to a hollow where juniper bushes exuded heat, spreading their branches like chickens brooding. Here I would lie on soft layers of fallen needles and scratch the chalky skin from the juniper berries with my thumb-nail. I could hear a trickle of water, the dream-like buzz of insects, a patter of nuts that fell without apparent reason from the tree-tops. I listened to the passing of leaf over leaf, the sweet, endless rustle of summer.

It was as if the trees were beings of another order, grave, aloof, and that they were aware of me and accepted me, even though I was a visitor in a community to which I did not belong.

From the junipers, a narrow animal trail wound down into a grove of young sugar maples. Sunlight, shimmering with pollen and the shine of insect wings, shafted down through openings in the trees, and the trail vanished under glades of feathery green ferns. I could tell where it was, though, a subtle snake of darkness where small animals had parted the fern stems.

I walked down this trail quickly, waist-deep in the green fronds. The ferns, the trees, the soil under my sneakers were as familiar to me as a suburban child's neighborhood; I felt the ferns brush the palms of my hands as another child might run a stick along a picket fence.

Just beyond the sugar maples, in a corner of the woods, I strayed off the path and stumbled upon fifteen apple trees standing in rows. A hundred years ago, someone had planted them in an open field. But now the trees were dead, their bark was black, and tangly bunches of brittle twigs obscured their branches. The place was dank, the ground spongy with moss and pale mushrooms. Grape vines swarmed flagrantly, made a dense mat over the trees, circled their trunks, grappled, choked. The old trees were like some black creatures of nightmare, frozen in a malevolent crouch; and the green vines were vindictive, triumphant.

I couldn't imagine these trees covered with pink blossoms, or heavy-limbed with shining apples. I stopped on the edge of the ancient orchard; nothing could have made me go into that dark and twisted place. I darted back to the sunny ferns, and never again went near that corner of the woods alone. Yet I felt its presence the same way I knew the dark corners of our house. It was like the place all town children know not to go: the parking lot behind the railway station, the pedestrian tunnel in the park.

The path's winding familiarity was comforting in a place where patterns changed daily, where branches fell on windy nights, or leaves unfurled and cast new shadows. Where the ground was bare, I looked for the shell-like curves of deer hooves, or piles of rabbit scat, and I knew the animals were close, for the tracks were always

fresh. The path emerged in a clearing where there was a tiny, spring-fed pond. In the summer, dragonflies hovered over its surface, and turtles sunned on sticks that dropped from the branches of a massive oak tree. The oak stretched its branches over the pond, over the pasture beyond the wall, and was taller and broader than all the other trees, somnolent with age, a dominant monolith.

I thought of it as *my oak*.

I could see it from my bedroom window. In the winter, its mound of bare branches, complex as brain coral, etched the sky; in summer, it towered like a thundercloud. No longer pliant, it did not bend with the wind. Its trunk, like a river boulder, broke the current of air, but its brittle limbs shuddered, and after a storm, the ground was littered with broken branches like bones after a feast.

I climbed onto the stone wall, feeling the smaller rocks slip as I pushed with my sneakers, and pulled with my arms. My feet scrambled up the tree trunk into the lowest and heaviest branches, and I

was safe in the tree, high, hidden, as much a part of it as the wood-peckers, the bark beetles, the spiders and ants who nested or fed on it. Sometimes I would worm my way out onto the tip of one of these branches, straddling it; but more often I would wedge myself in a crotch of branch and bole, my legs crossed and my back against the wide trunk. Here I would sit, imagining myself in various adult roles, or brooding on injustice, knowing the oak in the thoughtless way we know those who are closest to us, details lost in a picture held so close we cannot see it.

I leaned against the hard bark that knobbed my back. I did not wonder why this tree was still standing when so many of its contemporaries had been cut for lumber or firewood. It didn't occur to me that a tree could have a purpose other than simply to be alive, just as I did not wonder, yet, what my purpose should be.

The oak, *my oak*, was no more than what I imagined it to be. I put my hand on its deeply grooved bark, whenever I arrived or left, and whispered greetings and good-byes to it. Sometimes I cried a child's tears, and pressed my wet cheek, or a small hand, to its stolid trunk. I hung talismans in its branches. But the comfort came from my own act; the tree—branches, leaves, stems, veins, capillaries, roots, sap—simply grew, and went on growing, in the same place, season after season. Birds made nests and left, and the nests rotted and tumbled away; generations of cows browsed in the pasture; the cabin my brother and I built of an old packing crate moldered and fell inward, and was lost under thistles and couch grass; and under the tree's branches, the pond became choked with reeds and dried up. Turtles moved away, there were no more frogs, no peepers in the spring. And still the oak grew.

The comfort that the oak itself gave me, regardless of my whisperings or talismans, was comfort of another, wild kind: the knowledge that until wind or a chainsaw determined otherwise, the tree would remain. When I returned from the life I would go away to live, it would still be here on the hill. When I died, the oak would be catching powder snow on its gray branches, and its brown leaves would be rattling on the winter wind.

The haunted orchards of childhood hover, always, at the edges of summer days. Every place, it seemed, had its pocket of darkness, its kernel of terror, even the back of my closet. But the oak was one place I could trust, one place of complete safety, one place I could hide. And I sensed, at the tree's heart, terror's opposite, the sap of life untouched by corruption.

ARTIFACTS

In New Brunswick, I soon learned "bush" means something quite

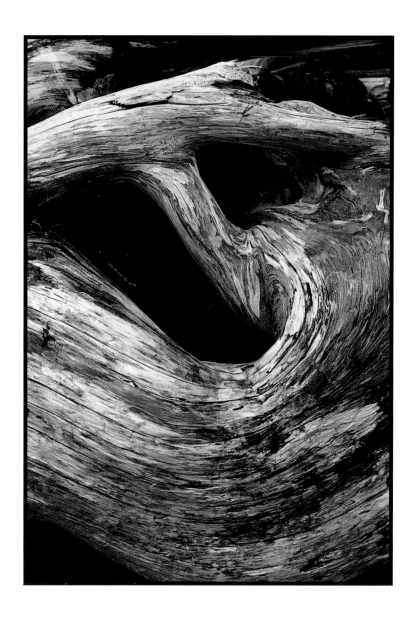

TREES

different from the lilac, rhododendron, forsythia, or hydrangea bushes of the south.

New Englanders do talk about bushwhacking, meaning to leave a path and find your own way through the trees; but bush, as wilderness, was something I had not encountered until I came north. To "go in the bush" sounded odd, to my ears, like floundering in the branches of a vast garden shrub. But this, it seemed, was what it was like to be in an apparently endless forest, as if you had become tiny and found yourself clambering about in a world of leaves, twigs, and insects.

In cities, we learn to pinpoint location by remembering businesses, parks, buildings: this is the block with the coffee shop, this is the street with the museum. In the country, we read trees. Here is the stretch with the poplar stands. This is the place with the third-growth fir, so dense not even a deer could force its way through. There, exposed to the wind, are the gray maples, stumpy, like miniature trees. Here, for miles, is a plantation, row on row of spruce trees, all the same age. There are the tamaracks, twisting out of the marsh, yellow-needled in November.

The predominant sound, in a forest, is made by trees; they rush and roar against the air, restless as the sea. Trees transmute the hillsides, subtle as chameleons, shifting endlessly through the spectrum, hard gray in winter, soft pink in spring. On summer nights the air is sharp with spruce resin; in autumn, when the hills are hidden behind hanging clouds, every water drop carries the scent of leaf mold, of decay and rebirth.

At first, learning a new land, I did not connect the smell of the forest with my tea kettle spurting steam on the wood stove. The pervasive essence of trees was not yet part of my concept of home, like the geraniums on the windowsill, like toast, or wooden spoons. The woods were far away beyond the fields; our house sat solitary in the grass, every tree banished, except for the maples which stood like schoolchildren at the edge of the lawn.

One morning, that first summer, I leaned in the doorway of the farmhouse, hands around a mug of tea, watching the sun rise over the spruce trees. I decided to take the morning off, to head out over the fields and explore the woods. I thought I'd take a book with me, and prop myself against a tree: read for a while, perhaps, by a stream.

The woods were rough, ragged, impassable in places. Most of the firs were dead or dying, their bud tips hollowed out spring after spring by an epidemic of budworm. The weakened trees went down easily in winter storms. Dead firs piled across one another like Lincoln Logs, and gray beard moss claimed the carcasses. I couldn't walk; I scrambled. Save for the logging roads, or clearings where forgotten piles of logs rotted into the soil, there were no easy paths. I tripped on fallen branches, slipped on half-buried mossy rocks. Crouched, arms pushing aside alders, I fought my way along a stream that emptied into a marsh, blackflies chewing my neck and clinging to the soft skin behind my ears. There were animal trails everywhere, but they overlapped, making a wandering, directionless maze that led into thickets too dense to enter.

I carried a backpack containing a paperback book and a thermos of tea. When I reached a grove of beech and maple on the first ridge, I stopped; it was high enough that I could see, if not the farms and fields of the valley below, at least the shining brightness of clear space. Panting, insect-bitten, scratched, I leaned against a beech,

listening to the blood rush in my ears.

I looked at the bowl I had just climbed. Leaves rustled high above the slender trunks of young trees, the breeze made a flicker of light and shadow, fingering through the ferns; and I realized I could not distinguish this particular hollow from any other. I did not know the hillside where trillium grew, could not find the tree with the witch's butter, or the dried-up brook bed, or the place where the deer yarded.

If I continued, there would be more hardwood stands like this one, more close-standing spruce in damp river valleys, marshes spiked with dead trees, raspberry-choked clearings, old clear-cuts tossing with fireweed and bowled with a hard blue sky, and then a ridge of birch again, another clump of spruce, on and on with no center, no pattern, no beginning and no end.

The quiet became suspect, taunting, and I felt the cold edge of unknowing. I was afraid to go on, afraid to go over the next ridge.

Somewhere, deer stood frozen, waiting. Rabbits had gone to ground. Black bear, moose, foxes, coyotes, snakes: all knew, or so I felt, my exact place. All smelled my alien heat. All paused, sensing, waiting. The rustling of the leaves came in waves, as the wind ebbed and strengthened, capriciously. It was a sound that excluded me. It was not like the whish of wind coming through a screen door; it was without comfort, or reference.

This was a world of wariness; the soft-footed coyotes would flicker easily among the gray trunks, coats dappling, shifting, paws stealthy and silent; their quick steps would pick around this tree, steal down through the shadows of the bowl.

I had crossed a boundary. Even though I might see the remains of humans—clear-cuts, saw marks, barbed wire embedded in bark— this was a place that followed its own course as steadily as the rivers that flow beneath cities. The heart of these woods was hidden, buried deep. I could walk here, but until I had watched and listened, patiently, and without expectation or design, until then I would move as if through the corridors of a museum, viewing artifacts that my hands could not remember, my soul could not celebrate.

On this day, leaning exhausted and bewildered against the beech tree, I felt the weight of the forest and knew why the early people had removed it so far from their farms. I felt its danger; I understood its affront to human sensibility. This was not a place for us. I was alone here, and utterly without importance. This was not the somnolent paradise of my childhood. *The woods are to work in. You don't go walking there.* I rose abruptly and shouldered my pack, slipping, ducking, scrambling noisily as I picked my way down the hill. I felt my self, and confidence, returning, bit by bit, as my feet crunched along a gravel road made by humans, as I swung along the edges of fields, as I turned my back on the wild.

THE PATTERN OF THE FOREST

It was November, our first autumn on the farm. The ground was frozen, there were white crystals in the black ice on the pond, and the sun traveled low across the southern sky.

We went into the woods to cut next year's firewood.

We were up on the hardwood ridge. We had a tractor, a chainsaw, peavey, chains, a plastic bottle of red oil, gasoline. We wore striped cotton gloves with leather palms. We wore boots and wool jackets and fluorescent orange toques. We smelled of sap, of gasoline. Behind the tractor, a trailer was loaded with four-foot logs, lashed with chains.

It was late afternoon. The night cold came sharp with the lengthening of the shadows.

We stood in the reverberant, stunned emptiness that is the silence after the chainsaw. Only the branches rattled, trees that went on swaying as if unaware of the sap-wet stumps, the scatter of chips and red-stained sawdust strewn on the green moss and the fading leaves.

The chainsaw swung from my husband's hand easily, with casual and implicit power, like a rifle. We knew it was time to go home, but it is hard to stop, once you have begun slicing trees.

We were still seeing with predatory eyes: the straight ones, the branchless ones, the ones that would fall clean, the ones that would split nicely. Pigs can be viewed as bacon, and trees as firewood. We discovered how quickly this can happen, once we had felt the quality of the cold, had woken in a house with frost shards on the nail-heads.

Then we noticed the maple.

It stood in a little clearing made by its own claiming of light. It was disproportionately massive; like the oak of my childhood, it had somehow escaped the fate of its contemporaries. There were no branches for forty feet, and the trunk rose in a muscled twist, fluid winds graven in wood. All its branches spread above the forest ceiling, an intricate network that we could have seen from the house, had we known to look, the crown of a forest elder making a living link between this moment and the instant of the seed's sprouting, and proclaiming the simple and wondrous fact of endurance, of deep-rooted being.

But we saw only lumber. We saw maple counter-tops, protected by varnish. We saw a kitchen table. We saw shelves, where we could put our first, proud belongings. We imagined slabs of lumber, stacked to dry in the barn loft.

It was thus, armed, that we began our acquaintance with the woods that had become, by the stroke of a pen, *ours*.

We set to work quickly. Soon the western sky would flare red and a planet would appear, clear and white over the shadowed side of the hill.

Tomorrow we would return to limb the tree, and to haul it out. Tonight we would simply cut it down.

The night crept around us, like rising water, as my husband revved the saw and approached the tree. All around the clearing, the maples sighed, trembling slightly in the cold air. Up and down the hillside, as far as the eye could see, stood the silent trees, numerous beyond

counting, a grave and mysterious multitude. But I thought: *supper, tractor, diesel, go to the lumber yard, buy grain, clear the loft, bank account, chicken, winter squash and mashed potatoes.*

When the saw touched the tree's bark—a testing cut, the way the dentist presses your gum before inserting the needle—the crown of the tree swayed. It swayed, not as the other trees continued their gentle stirring, but in small, tremulous jerks.

The chainsaw whined, chewed. Its sound passed far across the valley, was heard by every farmer crossing his barnyard, by every child running across the frozen yards, by every creature in the otherwise soundless November evening.

The chain circled to stillness.

We backed far away from the tree, at a tangent to its path, looking up at its crown which still towered, as if unaffected.

The woods were completely silent, save for the whish of wind.

Then came the first creak.

Wordless, alone in the still air, a wrenching groan, the sound of a creature forced to articulation.

Then it stopped.

Again it came, the tearing creak, the groan of bursting sinews.

This time, the tree shuddered, staggered. Its branches lurched.

Once more, it was still. It was still for such a long time that we stepped tentatively towards it. Then, with a great, wracking split and scream the trunk swept forward, branches flung back like hair as the tree thundered downward falling faster, twisting, tearing with it smaller trees, a chaos of cracking branches and then, with a hardness, a mass beyond imagining, the trunk smashed into the ground with brutal finality. The ground quaked beneath our feet, and then there was a shower of falling branches, twigs, a long settling, and a terrible silence.

We did not move. In an instant, the twilight of the forest was gone, and we stood in an unnatural clearing. Above us, through the opening, the bald, unfiltered light of early evening poured into the woods, exposing secrets, dispelling mystery.

Except for the branches that continued to patter down, randomly, there was an intent stillness, as if the tree's falling were like a rock tossed into dark waters, and ripples spread out and out, into the taut ears of deer, or rabbits wide-eyed in their burrows, into dens, warrens, and nests, into the waters of the ice-edged brooks, into fiber and root, signifying a shift, an irreversible change in the pattern of the forest.

The maple had spent its long life reaching for the sky, growing always up, always vertical, striving to place its leaves in sunlight; at its crown, its branches made a twisty compromise between their own upward thrust and the northeast wind. Its gnarly twigs sprouted soft leaves; thrushes gripped its bark, fluting their songs down through the rustling green. In an instant, this sacred record of wind and weather, this home to birds, insects, fungi, system within system, as far beyond our comprehension as the plangent song of the whales: all this, and simply a tree, lay forever motionless on the ground, waiting for us to change it into something square, straight, and useful, or into fire and ash.

We had to leave the tree as a tree, that night. It was too dark to make it into neat stacks of logs, to effect the transformation that gave us such satisfaction, such sense of order.

We climbed onto the tractor. Peter put it in its lowest gear and we jolted slowly down a precipitous track that became a streambed in spring. The trailer lurched behind us, the chains shifting and clinking around the logs. We came out into the field; the pale grass held the light of the last bands of sunset still lying across the western sky, and I could see the dark bulk of house and barns down in the valley and a welcoming ribbon of smoke wisping from the chimney, something of my own against the cold sky.

We left the tractor and the trailer on the driveway outside the kitchen window. Taking my coat off in the unheated hall, stooping to unlace my boots, I liked the smell of bark and gasoline, I liked

the ache in my arms, and as I dropped an armload of logs into the woodbox and crunched a log into the stove and saw the yellow flames wreathing around the wood like a spirit, I accepted my part in the chain of events. We needed heat, we cut trees.

Then I thought of the maple lying in the darkness, its leaves slowly curling inward and becoming limp, its branches cracked and smashed.

LUMBER

It took us two full days to haul the maple out of the woods. We wanted the trunk intact, for lumber, and so we didn't cut it into sections but hauled it out as one mighty log. It was far too heavy for the tractor, which reared onto its back tires and nearly flipped. A chain broke and whipped past my head. Traversing a steep hill, the trunk of the tree began to roll sideways; the hauling chain caught in the tire lugs, nearly reeling the log into the wheel.

We took it out, however, every bit. We burned the branches in our stoves. We milled the trunk and used the lumber to make tables, counter tops, and shelves.

I always tell people that this bird's-eye maple around our sink comes from a tree we cut ourselves, from our own woods. What I do not tell was how, in the silence after the maple fell, I understood for the first time the extent of my own destructiveness; how I learned that with the flip of a finger I could take something away from the earth, forever. I do not describe how quickly I learned to enjoy my power, to think of trees as my own. I do not recount how my bones felt the shudder of the earth. I do not describe the silence.

Footpaths

Later, we began to go into the woods with no reason other than to learn the terrain, to make footpaths. We watched, we listened. Bits of knowledge made new shapes in our minds the way snowflakes change a landscape.

Mouse tracks in the snow, trails like tiny horseshoe crabs, linked, disappearing under the crust, coming up again.

Snow showering from the branches of spruce trees in a glistening flash of color, red, gold, silver.

The icy shock of water on my scalp, twigs and bits of moss in my hair, bathing naked in the waterfall.

Leaves, in October, wavering down and overlapping, red on yellow on green, and a spike of club moss.

A sea of Dutchman's breeches, hanging succulent, fragrant heads, not a garden for anyone's pleasure, simply there, stirring quietly, yellow faces a human would name *innocent*.

Golden beeches bending before the winds of autumn; leaves streaming, branches bouncing; wind like surf, a rising, expending, gathering roar.

Storms, darkness in the west, smell of snow at night; daybreak and the nearest line of spruces barely visible, lost in the swirling white.

The snarling scream of raccoons after dark; hoot of a great horned owl; sounds on the edge of dream.

The smell of trees coming into my kitchen, when I open the back door on a summer's morning.

All these things became part of me, and I began to understand the sharp loveliness of the woods, and that they were not there for me, or for anyone else.

DAYBREAK

Twenty years after the cutting of the great maple I am sitting in the same woods. It is spring. A breeze ruffles the leaves, the mists disperse. I am watching daybreak in the forest.

I sit on a hillside watching a brook tumble over twenty feet of mossy cliff. At the lip, the water is sinewy and black, sliding over the moss, but then it tips free, froths down in a spume of white bubbles. It splashes into a pool, continues, pool after pool, tiny silvery falls descending between the trees.

Where I sit, all the trees are conifers, and it's damp, there's not much undergrowth and the needly soil is strewn with twigs; across from me, on the eastern hillside, the trees are hardwoods, gray-barked, white-barked, their leaves just unfurling. Beneath them, red trillium turn star-shaped faces to the brown carpet of last year's leaves.

A white-throated sparrow calls. The notes fade away; then it calls again, and again.

The woods are light, open. It is the time between snow and the verdancy of summer. I have walked carefully, avoiding spring beauty, wood anemones, yellow violets, the tiny flowers of early spring.

The sun shimmers up through the trees. There is a quickening, a quivering of prismatic light around every leaf.

My eye catches movement. I see silver strands floating in the air, high over the brook. They descend from the branches of trees. They catch and then lose the light. They cross, float, drift. Gossamer, iridescent, they are sticky silk, lines cast by hundreds of hunting spiders who know that here, in the morning light and the rising currents of air, they will find insects.

I'm not part of this world of the forest. Unlike the spiders, no instinct informs me; I listen to the complex arguments of my brain and cannot hear the darker, deeper messages. I would not know, as does this great gathering of spiders, that this is the precise place I must spin my web and cast my line.

I sit with my chin in my hands, gazing upward. And just for an instant, my busy brain folds its wings and is still, and I feel the spiders' world. The forest morning pierces my humanness. I see the dignity, the urgency, the thrill of the shimmering strands. I'm humbled by spiders; swept to the edge of mystery.

And I'm as alive, in this cool forest, as I was as a child, when my sweet-smelling woods were more home than home; when I could feel safe in the mighty branches of my oak.

❦

TREES

WILD PLANTS

"Be grateful for impermanence and the freedom
it grants us. For in a fixed universe
there would be no freedom . . .
the wild, as the process and essence of nature,
is also an ordering of impermanence."

GARY SNYDER

WILD PLANTS

Summer scrapes the heels of spring. One day you wear your wool jacket and there's snow in the shadows. The next, it seems, the daffodils are drying at the edges, and baby swallows clamor in their nests.

It is June, dusk, and I am reluctant to go into the house. Light drains from the sky, and I stand in the gathering darkness and feel another day slip past.

In the evening, the hollow, mournful wing-song of snipes traverses the sky long after the other birds have sought refuge and fallen silent. Like owls, peepers, and bats, snipes are stirred by darkness. I look up, but can never see them; and so their winnowing weaves invisibly across the blue-black sky with a loveliness that wavers between joy and anguish, like family faces candlelit at a celebration.

A band of red light flushes the northwest, fading slowly as embers, and on the ridge the spruce trees are crisp as black paper. Down here in the valley, I can't see the daisies and buttercups; they've been absorbed by the shadows, and the irises are pale as dream flowers. I smell freshly mown grass and honeysuckle. I listen to the rhythmic, silvery throb of peepers, over in the marsh.

The transformation happens gradually, without distinction; at no instant can I say the day has ended, night has begun. Yet one thing goes, and another takes its place. The green leaves of the hawthorn become shadow. The red-feathered chickens turn black, and the black horse vanishes, is no more than the sound of teeth tearing grass. Like the snipes, the brooks are distinct, lacing the darkness.

I open my hands and let another day fly free, release it like the sparrow hawk that I found flailing its wings frantically against the barn

window. One minute it was in my hands, fierce, heart racing; the next, a speck over the woods.

I go into the kitchen. Electric lights make a stage; night becomes our audience.

I wish I didn't have to sleep, to punctuate my life by the oblivion that slices one day from the one that came before. I leave all the doors and windows open, so that the night can breathe through the house, moonlight sweeping the kitchen floor, the smell of roses edging the breeze that carries the trill of peepers through the motionless rooms. The summer's rhythm is unbroken; time is marked not by day or night, but by the passing of one flower and the birth of another, by the deepening of the frogs' night chorus, by dandelions shifting from stolid yellow dots to shimmering silver, shattered by the slightest breeze.

The passing of summer is the passing of beauty. First the dandelions are gone. Next the daisies are gone. Now the fireweed has faded.

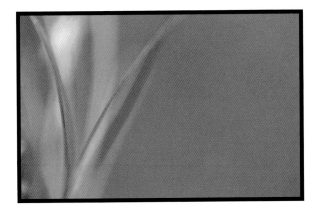

I feel the summer rushing towards me, falling away behind. I want to gather it, to hold on to it, but it sweeps past as steadily as my child's childhood, my parents' youth.

THE WILD GARDEN

Wildflowers proliferate, and grow in masses; lupins cover the banks of New Brunswick highways, mile after mile of blowing blue spires, and fireweed fills abandoned meadows. Sometimes, though, a clump of violets grows all by itself, in a forest clearing where the sun breaks in. The purple flowers on an isolated clump are lush, like a Victorian posy clustered in a child's hand. In its chance separation from the other violets, it propagates extravagantly, as if starting a new bed.

Even in a single plant there is a multitude, form repeating form in echoed curves, tiny sweeping lines swaying on the same breeze, stems lifting and bending, dense as jungle.

In early spring, the woods are moist; trees rise from a fecund floor of brown, sodden leaves. There's a sense of space. Bars of shadow alternate with shafts of watery sunlight. There's a green haze overhead, a mist of new leaves, and the tips of spruce and fir trees are bright green, like cats' paws. Mayflower, trout lily, Dutchman's breeches are soft, succulent, pushing through the winter's mulch, and they stir in the breeze, as delicate as the young leaves, high above.

Wherever there's a clearing, bunchberries spread out from under the dark skirts of spruce trees. The pink-veined white carpet offers coherence, simplicity within the random chaos of fallen trees and tangled branches; it radiates peace and settled warmth. The sturdy flowers grow close, petal overlaps petal, and the wild garden basks quietly in the sun for anyone who might come by: me, north-bound geese, pine grosbeaks, a rambling bear.

Spring wildflowers can't be picked; they're as ephemeral as the season itself. I've arrived home with limp trout lilies in the palm of my hand. They cannot bear separation from the soil.

I say to myself, *This year I won't miss the first flowers*, and even so, I will miss them. It might rain for a few days, and the painted trillium will be battered, translucent as wasp wings. Or I go away for a week, and never see the fiddleheads unfurl, or miss the coltsfoot entirely.

The flowers appear, and blossom, and toss in the wind, and fade, and shrivel, year after year, as predictably as the wheeling stars. Just as we can say, *Now is the time Orion's belt is over the roof*, so we say, *It's the time of rhodhora* or *The lupins are blooming*. We're navigating summer; we know what lies behind, and what is still to come.

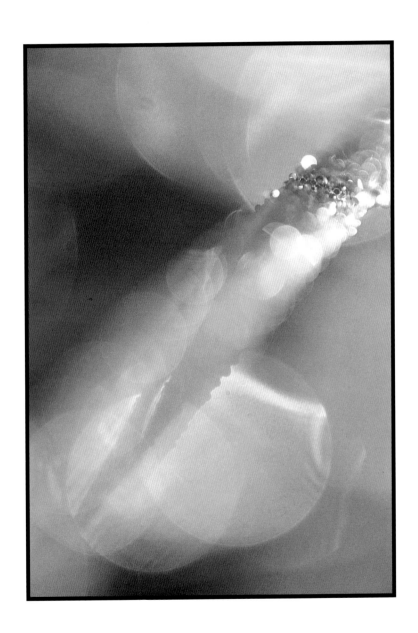

WILD PLANTS

Spring flowers emerge subtly, and go unnoticed, like the solitary fluting of a wood thrush. But the summer flowers sweep over the open hills, claim meadows, and crowd river banks like a rollicking flock of blackbirds.

First, the fields green. The rain is itself a sign; it's not just rain but *the greening rain*, cause for celebration, washing away the last ribs of snow splayed along the edge of the woods. Then fruits set flowers; wind-lashed cherries scatter white petals over the new green grass, while on the banks of the pond wild strawberries offer their yellow pollen to the bees. Low-bush blueberries sprawl on rock cairns, pink blossom warmed by gray stone.

House-dwellers can't be expected to keep up with every leaf's unfurling. Still, I feel I've missed some essential moment when, dropping pancake batter into the frying pan, I look out the south window and notice that the bank along the brook is misted with a froth of rhodhora, pink flowers sprouted miraculously from a tangle of brittle branch.

WILD PLANTS

Rhodhora are the first of the summer flowers that bloom in such profusion that the landscape is transformed. As I flip a pancake oozing with frozen blueberries and squint through the blue smoke of burning butter, I know that wildflower season is here.

There will be flowers until frost, but what I call wildflower season is the time when the flowers are neither spring-fragile, nor tough and fibrous like the ocherous blooms of fall. Within themselves they're balanced between wet and dry, sap and strength. It's midsummer, a long time since snow-melt, and a long time until the first frost, and the flowers bloom insouciantly, with carefree extravagance under the high white clouds of July. It seems as if this time of balsam-scented sunrise and massed daisies, of wet towels on the line after swimming and voices in the summer evening, will go on and on, durable as the bouquets of daisies, vetch, and clover that last for days in Mason jars on bureaus in bedrooms.

The weather is settled. Every morning I wake to the same dappled sky, the chatter of swallows, and spider webs hanging in the fields

like gray veils that are transformed into sparkling silver scarves as the sun rises. *When the spiders make webs, the day will be fine.* Day after day, the pasture is a sea of yellow buttercups; on my way to the mailbox I see mounds of wild mint and blue forget-me-nots along the dwindling brook. There are daisies, all the same height, rippling up the hillsides, and so much clover, pink and white, that I can smell it from the back porch. I'm drinking iced tea with my neighbor's daughters, and the swinging couch creaks on its chains while they tell me about the lupin battles of their childhood; how they'd strip handfuls of the blue blossoms and hurl them into the bright air, over the schoolyard fence.

Abundance: of time, of flowers. There's something about this excess that makes me want both to squander and to gather.

I want to live these perfect days free of the knowledge that they will never come again. I want to watch children in this moment of their childhood, balanced, like the flowers, between extremes. I want to squander time, let it pass unregretted, ungathered.

Yet I pick the flowers. I can't bear not to. There are so many daisies that I could pick a bunch as big as a sheaf of wheat. They appeared without anguish or struggle. They are there for the picking; for what other reason?

One day I notice that the swallow's nest in the woodshed is empty. Leaves are faded, and there's more wind. Sheets snap on the line. The neighbors don't come swimming at the pond. The Yellow Transparent is covered with apples. Raccoons start haunting the edges of the fields. Goldenrod nods dusty at the roadsides, brown galls in their stems, and down in the meadow, where it seems I just noticed the flag iris, there is blue aster, instead.

Summer is like a shadow; turn and it is gone.

I pick bouquets of steeplebush, goldenrod, pussytoes. This is the last wave, the last and most subtle tapestry of summer, dusty blue touched with red, yellow brushed with the white of seed fluff.

Even in this season of desiccation there is a freely given harvest, multitudes of repeated forms. Yet even as I gather the last autumn flowers, I poison the apple-scented days with my own regret, my own sense of standing at the edge of every moment, reaching out, unable to catch something important that always gets away.

SEEDS OF ANOTHER SUMMER

Some seeds simply dry and drop. Others drift afield on white, wind-catching fluff.

The thistles are packed to bursting with thousands of seeds, each on its own silken aerial. In September, the seeds erupt from tough, spiny sacs and spin into the air, twirling, catching on spider webs, barbed wire, wool sleeves. They sail high into the sky and vanish like migrating birds.

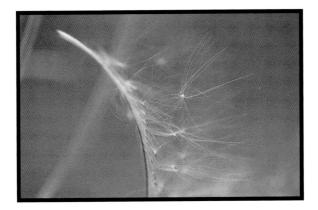

The wind carries them, and when the air stills, the seeds settle to earth, gently.

The cycle begins again, perhaps in Russell Wilkins' pasture, perhaps down in Waterford. Perhaps across the bay. Who knows? Contained in each seed that every flower casts to the wind, or drops to the soil, is that flower's shape, color, scent. All winter, through freeze and thaw, the brilliant flux of color, the tossing flower faces, lie dormant.

The seeds of another summer wait, under the snow.

❦

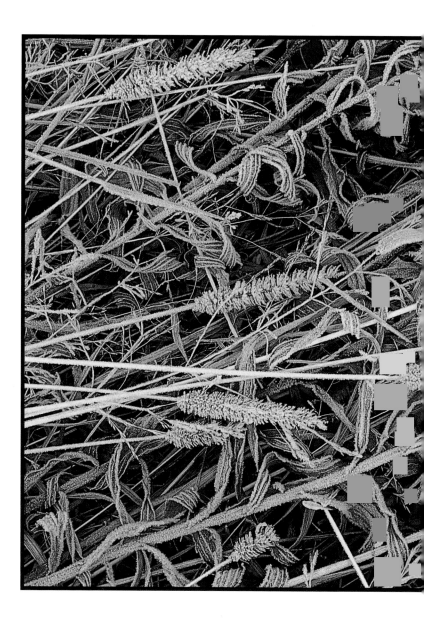

H O M E

"The vast wild
      the house, alone.
The little house in the wild,
      the wild in the house.
Both forgotten.

              No nature

        Both together, one big empty house."

                GARY SNYDER

H O M E

Home, this place where I live, is like a soft leaf on a great tree.

On clear summer mornings, I like to come downstairs, barefoot, and stand in the kitchen, stretching, yawning. Through open windows I watch light shining in the tall timothy grasses which stir like a restless sea all around the house.

It is my twenty-fifth summer here.

The comfortable, homey chirp of swallows and the snipes' mournful, swooping wing-whistle are the sounds of early morning, familiar as water filling a kettle. Wind swishes softly, endlessly, in the maples. I smell the dry-wood, old farmhouse smell of wood smoke and mice; and daisies, their bitter scent riding a dancing breeze. Sun lies in a warm oblong on the wide pine floorboards. Hiking boots are tumbled by the wood stove, shedding sand from the beach we walked on yesterday, along the Bay of Fundy, under cliffs layered with the earth's past, and bored by the dark holes of cliff swallows.

I can't imagine ever leaving this place.

I put a loaf of oatmeal bread on the kitchen table, slice down through it. The wooden table is criss-crossed with thin knife scars, like smile lines on a man's cheek. A cat mews at the screen door, just beneath the swallows' nest in the woodshed, and I hear the small thunder of wings as the parent birds swoop through the open shed door to harangue the cat.

Home. Would I ever have the energy to start again, to come drifting into an unknown place like a vagrant seed? I've taken root and accepted the demands of this world. I'm growing, like my own garden that responds to all the particular elements of this valley; long summer days, cold nights, altitude, wind, the distant presence of the sea. I've become what this valley has made me.

My life, and where I live it, can't be separated, like the trout lily that can't bear separation from the soil. I've become a leaf on a tree. I'm connected to a greater whole.

I take my breakfast outside, sit on the back step, and look down the green, blowing valley. Towels flap on the line. It'll be a good day to make hay. *Clear out the hay mow, remember to take the baby gift over to Laura, pull up the spinach.*

Suddenly, like a hawk on a slipstream, I'm swept away. Looking down the valley, bread and marmalade in hand, my experience of this rough and peaceful place runs through me like a current. Twenty-five years of memories are woven into the rushing of the wind, the shining of the grasses. *My neighbor bawling hymns over the drone and clatter of his tractor as he cuts hay. Children sauntering down the road whack-ing dusty flower heads with sticks. Meetings in our living room, with fervent and heated discussions on how we would improve many things. Me, weeping, heartbro-ken, face in hands. Twenty people at a sawhorse-and-plank table, one Thanksgiving, sitting on upended logs before we had any chairs. Children rampaging like a storm blowing through the house. Bringing my infant son home from the hospital, his head like a soft flower in my hand on just such a shining day.*

The ache of homesickness has become a distant memory; a sorrow buried deep.

The moment passes. How often do we experience sheer happiness? So rarely that it's a feeling I examine and then recognize, like an old friend met unexpectedly. I wipe jammy fingers on my jeans, smiling, shaking my head slightly.

I walk around the house and go in through the back door. The swallows dart in ahead of me. I wonder if the brown barn spider, with fine, ash-gray hairs on her long legs, will return this August, angling her web across the door frame so we have to duck when we enter.

We can't shut the back door of our house. Other creatures need it. The wild has come in.

The Larger Darkness of Night

Home is like a leaf on a tree; other people, other homes, are the other leaves. They live beneath the same sky, share the same memories, survive the same storms.

But one leaf is a solitude.

Although I laugh, comfort people, am hugged by those who love me, still and always, I'm alone. Sometimes I feel as frail as the seeds I drop into my garden furrows. We go through life carrying with us a profound ignorance of our own beginnings, our own ends. I imagine myself curled inside my mother. I imagine my body as bits of mineral, ash and bone, smoking on the wind.

We're all leaves, growing on a tree so vast we can barely imagine it: a tree as infinite and encompassing as the larger darkness of night.

Our homes surround us, strong and safe as a snail's convoluted shell or a turtle's dark casing. Home becomes home not only when we've added comforts—soft rugs, tablecloths, paintings, geraniums—but when we've made our lives dense with family and friends, and spun memories like spiders.

The world we inhabit, with its skies, rivers, rocks, trees, storms, stars, also surrounds us, a carapace of another sort that extends far beyond the walls of our houses. It is the tree we can't see. It's our

larger home; a home that supports us, just as the bole of a tree carries sap to its leaves.

We make ourselves aliens in a strange place if we choose not to hear its languages, or to see its messages. The land seems a fearful place to those who live inattentively. This is how it seemed to me when we moved to this farm, and I saw the black press of night beyond the wet glass of our bedroom window on our first night. I heard the language of crickets and birds and thought it had nothing to do with me; I couldn't read the meaning of the new position of the stars over the barn, and didn't understand the exuberant message of the sound of the brook in spate.

But just as I feel at home, now, in my valley, meshed in my memories, so I begin to sense the presence of the great tree, like a reality behind reality. The longer I live here on earth, the more I love the light of sunrise, the silent tumble of snow from motionless branch, mute raven's track in mud, moonset at dawn over a field of silky grasses, sleeping cows, spiders, thin trickling of the world's water.

Now, after all these years, I'm becoming literate in the other language. My feet know the twist of knobby spruce roots. My hands caress soft moss beds. I've smelled leaf mold on autumn mist, tasted sun-hot blueberries. And occasionally, as I touch, taste, and listen, the boundary between nature and me becomes a threshold: I step across. The wild either slips into me, or comes leaping up, like a silver fish, flashing out of my own dark wildness.

WILDFLOWERS OF WINTER

February tenth.

I'm longing for a blizzard. Without storms, winter creeps by dully, undelineated, and I become irritable. Storms are like the wildflowers of winter; they mark the passage of time, restore perspective and scale.

A thin, milky layer of cloud creeps across the sky, and the sun becomes pale, without presence. I smell snow on the air, and hear, on the radio, that a storm is approaching from Quebec.

All day, I wait, anticipating. The temperature drops. The air is very still. At suppertime, my son declares he doesn't need to do his homework, there won't be school.

At bedtime, I take Hooper, our terrier, for her nightly pee. As I slide open the glass door of the sunroom, she pushes past me and then stops abruptly; she squints her eyes and lifts her nose to the wind. I follow her outside.

133

HOME

It is snowing hard.

The small flakes swirl on a northeast wind and it is very quiet. Out in the darkness, a barely audible whistling begins, a steel whine in the branches of the trees. It's a sound I've heard before. I know it the way a sailor knows the meaning of the wind in the rigging. The dog knows it too; she has her pee under the lilac bush and comes right back.

In the light from the kitchen window, I can see snow swirling around the broken stalks of phlox in the garden; already there's a place where the snow begins to gather, a tiny, sinuous curve defining the massive drift that always forms in the lee of the house.

According to the kitchen thermostat, the temperature has dropped four degrees since supper. I take down the transistor radio from its shelf so we can listen to the school report tomorrow without getting out of bed. I stand in the darkness and think about the barn, the animals, the tractor, all the things and creatures asleep or still in the night while forces build around us, pressure drops, wind rises, cold increases.

Suddenly, the wind buffets the house and there's an icy whisper, a handful of tiny diamonds flung against the black windows.

I go upstairs and undress in the same northwest room where we spent our first night in this house, when we slept on a damp mattress huddled under rugs. Tonight, the bed is warm, it's a nest that my body knows. I roll into it and pull the quilt high over my shoulders. I listen to the rising, roaming wind, hear the icy tap of snow against the window. I can hear the furnace rumbling in the cellar. I feel myself gathered by the dark wings of sleep and I drift easily, knowing that the storm is rising, glad that no one can stop it.

Many Voices

Sometime in the night we wake, Peter and I, at the same time. We lie silently, listening.

The wind is a full-force gale that rages across the open fields, encountering nothing until it slams into the house. It speaks in many voices, making a hollow liquid moan at corners, shrieking as it streams unimpeded over the roof. A lifted section of steel roofing bangs insistently. The house feels like a ship; it has come alive. The bed trembles.

We go downstairs and slide open the glass door. Instantly the noise is deafening, vast as the boom and crash of surf, a wild sustained howl. Across the darkness, the wind and the snow race and twist like maddened horses.

SNOWBOUND

The next morning, we waken to a muted light. It's like being inside an ice cave. We can't see anything out any of the windows except swirling snow. The maples at the edge of the lawn have become gray brushwork, steel-wool scrapings in the white-out. The wind still pummels the house, still rages down from the northwest.

When we go downstairs we find the cats pressed against the glass door, their whiskers frosted, their mouths open in piteous mews that we can't hear. When I open the door to let them in, the vast roar and twisting whine of the wind is suddenly in our kitchen, and snow blows onto the geraniums.

The radio tells us that a low pressure system is stalled over the Maritimes.

I go outside to tend the animals in the barn. I pull my hood up. The plastic toggle on the drawstring whips in the wind, hits me in the eye. I lean on the wind and watch my feet coming forward and forward, the only color in the whiteness. Already, between the house and the barn, there's a drift deeper than my knees.

In the barn, snow sifts through cracks in the north wall. The horse and the pony have snow on their eyelashes, on their coarse manes and in the grooves along their spines. They move restlessly about their stalls; the black mare tosses her nose impatiently. I brush snow off the hay bales, fill their mangers. When I stamp back into the boot-hall, I'm panting, my face is wind-whipped, dripping wet. I lean forward and shake snow out of my hair.

I spend most of the day curled in the corner of the couch, reading, drinking tea. Hours pass with no change in the intensity of the snow or the wind. We go to the windows, report to one another on the drifts which grow wherever the wind is checked. Snow streams steadily off the crests of the drifts, and their knife-edge lips become sharper and thinner, then begin to curl like fortune cookies.

By late afternoon the weather forecasters are predicting the biggest storm in fifty years.

The house hums with current: the refrigerator and the freezer whir, hot air pulses from the ducts, music plays from the stereo. Nonetheless, we search through drawers for candles and stick them into whatever we can find—beer bottles, glass jars. I rummage in the pantry for kerosene lamps and place the box of "strike anywhere" matches on the kitchen table. We fill the tub with water. Just in case.

At seven o'clock we lose power. It is a swift failing. One minute the

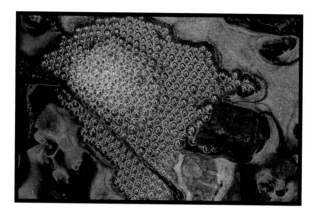

house is humming, ticking, clocks keeping track of time, electronic seconds pulsing on the VCR, we're spinning through the storm in our spaceship, warm, comfortable, and then the lights shut down, not the way they go when you click them off, but a swoop, a diminishment. A failure. A power failure.

First there is the darkness. It is pitch dark. Then there is the absence of any sound but the wind, and the flicking of snow against the windows. I see the line of red light around the lid of the cook stove, hear the quiet snap of the fire. I pick up the telephone, but it is dead. A piece of white plastic in my hand.

We light the candles. Shadows flicker on the walls as candle flames leap and shrink in the cold drafts. The only heat comes, now, from the kitchen stove, and the rest of the house gets cold, rapidly. It's quiet, *so quiet*—there are no distractions. Only the reflection of candles in the black windows, the snapping of the fire and the unceasing rage of the storm, the wild howl and moan, the rampaging of the wind.

All of us, mother, father, son, dog, and two cats, come to the kitchen. We come to the room where there is fire. By the stove are two buckets of water and a ladle. Steam wheezes gently from the kettle's spout. We bring a book and pass it around, taking turns reading out loud. Often we stop to listen to the storm.

Nothing compels us to do anything else. Nothing pulls us, fractures us.

We wavered when the power died, caught in actions half-completed, all our choices gone. In that instant, we were people in amber, caught between times; and now we return to something barely conceivable. People without power.

There's a particularly heavy buffet of wind, and the house shudders on its foundation.

Our senses are shaken awake, to shadows, shelter, measured words. To one another. The storm holds us; we have no control over our situation, and yet we are not diminished but wrapped in the mystery of wind, of shadows, of water in a bucket.

The boundary vanishes. We cross the threshold, and glimpse how we, too, are part of the night's world, the storm's song.

Nothing is so freeing as being snowbound.

Winter's Silence

It snows all the next day. Then, just at dusk, the wind dies, the clouds thin. Light comes into the rooms of the house, the humble light of late afternoon, when a sheen of cloud cannot mask the blue sky.

I pull open the wooden door at the end of the entry hall and am met with a neat wall of blue snow, as high as my chest. I take down my grandmother's snowshoes, work the toes of my boots under the leather thongs, buckle the straps.

I clamber up onto the snow and walk out into the evening.

A star hangs over the ridge. There's not a breath of wind. In the west, the sky is the color of apricots, dusky orange fading to the pink of a conch shell; and high above the valley, the sky is the softest blue, darkening in the east where the moon is rising.

As if it has been here forever, the snow lies serenely, its separate flakes flashing with the dying light. Drifts curl like frozen combers, pure, wind-shaped.

Nothing moves. The valley lies buried under snow, just the way the storm left it, and great swells obliterate the road.

It is silent save for the dry shirring of snow on snow, shifting in a tendril of air. No cars, no airplanes, no tractors. Not even the beat of a raven's wings.

My snowshoes carry me over the drifts. I stride over the buried garden fence and stand on top of the raspberries. I watch the sun setting, feel it flushing my cheeks, see the snow turning rose-red and blue shadows pooling along the porch.

Someone lights a candle inside the house. I watch its tiny flame move from room to room.

I stand there for a long time, feeling myself blending into the night as the hills darken around me, as stars prick the sky.

No lights shine from our house.

Our small, human home is an element of winter's silence, as indistinguishable from the black sky as a rock or a tree. It becomes, simply, another creature that lives on the great home of earth; and its bulk folds gradually into the darkness, like a black horse grazing at night.

⟡

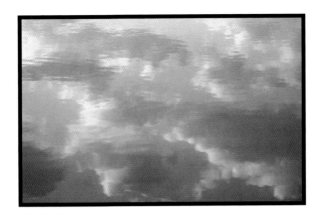

143

HOME

Book Design: Melanie Random
Editors: Jackie Kaiser, Mary Kalamaras
Copy Editors: Wendy Thomas, Enid Stubin
Production: Alice Wong, Christopher Young
Printed and bound in Singapore